Praise for *Before Amen:* *The Power of a Simple Prayer*

"Max Lucado has been an inspirational and spiritual leader for my family and me for many years. If you've never heard him speak, you need to. If you've never read one of his books, read this one. I promise, you will be inspired."

— George Strait, member,
Country Music Hall of
Fame

"*Before Amen* has a winning combination of simplicity and depth. This book is appropriate for people who struggle to pray and for all who long to pray more effectively. Max's 'pocket prayer' is brief but comprehensive; it helps readers turn to the Lord quickly and easily—in all circumstances. *Before Amen* is practical, enjoyable, and inspiring."

— Sarah Young,
best-selling and award-
winning author of *Jesus
Calling* and *Jesus Today*

"So many books on prayer make it seem daunting and complicated. This one makes it simple, clear, and childlike—which, after all, was Jesus' point."

— Philip Yancey, author,
*Prayer: Does It Make Any
Difference?*

"A new book by Max is like going back to your favorite restaurant. You know it's going to be delicious because it never disappoints. And *Before Amen* is a perfect next book for Max. The deeper he goes into the Word, the more crystallized and simple his message becomes. Delicious, satisfying, and always nourishing. Like good food, you'll grow from it."

> — Kathie Lee Gifford,
> cohost, the fourth hour
> of the *Today Show*

"If you know that prayer is important but often struggle to seek God consistently—this book is for you. In *Before Amen*, Max Lucado will not only lead you to want to pray more but will show you the power of simplicity in taking your needs before God."

> — Craig Groeschel, senior
> pastor, LifeChurch.tv;
> and author, *FIGHT:*
> *Winning the Battles that*
> *Matter Most*

"My friend Max Lucado has given us one of the finest practical tools for understanding, utilizing, and experiencing the power of prayer that has ever been written. In *Before Amen* you will be encouraged and inspired to make communicating with your heavenly Father a way of life."

> — Dr. Tony Evans,
> president and founder,
> The Urban Alternative;
> and senior pastor, Oak
> Cliff Bible Fellowship

"No one draws in my heart as a reader like Max Lucado. I've waited for years for him to write on prayer and when I read *Before Amen*, it was everything I'd hoped it would be. If you want your prayer life to come alive like never before, read Max's simple yet profound insights in this book. One of my top ten reads for 2014!"

— Lysa TerKeurst, *New York Times* best-selling author, *Unglued*; and president, Proverbs 31 Ministries

"When Max Lucado writes, he gets my sit-up-straight attention. And his words on prayer are some of the most riveting and poignant I've read. Max shows us how prayer is simple yet powerful, momentary yet eternity-changing. We all need this book."

— Rich Stearns, president, World Vision US; author, *The Hole in Our Gospel* and *Unfinished*

"If you feel uncertain in your prayer life, you're in good company. Max Lucado confesses to his own prayer failings. But there's hope for all who want to experience more fire and fervency when they talk with God. The answer isn't complex or intimidating. It's simple. Simple prayer. In *Before Amen*, Max joins readers on a path toward a confident, biblically based prayer life, one line—one phrase—at a time. Take this journey with him and discover the power and peace that comes from a true connection with God."

— Mark Batterson, *New York Times* best-selling author, *The Circle Maker*; and lead pastor, National Community Church

"There is nothing more powerful than a prayer. Our hopes, dreams, fears, and failures are changed, altered, and redeemed through simple prayers. My dear friend Max has taken the simplicity of prayer and revealed the dynamic power we have through communication with our Lord. May the request of the disciples in Luke 11:1 be our heart's cry: 'Lord, teach us how to pray.'"

— Christine Caine, founder,
The A21 Campaign; and
best-selling author of
Undaunted

"If you struggle with your prayer time as I do, you will love how simple, yet profound, Max's book and prayer guide is. No matter how much time you spend in prayer each day, this little book will make the most of that time. Follow this book and you will connect with God like never before. Thank you, Max!"

— Stephen Arterburn,
founder and chairman,
New Life Ministries;
best-selling author; and
host, New Life Live!

"Max on prayer! I can't think of a more inspiring author to show us how to pray better, stronger, and with more passion. Read *Before Amen* to take your prayer life to the next level and begin to see God's power flow through your life."

— Jack Graham, pastor,
Prestonwood Baptist
Church

"I really didn't intend to read *Before Amen* in one sitting. But the fact that I did reveals how much I needed to learn about this discipline with which we all struggle. Max clearly explains the components of prayer and in so doing makes me want to talk to God more regularly and conversationally."

> — Dave Stone, pastor,
> Southeast Christian
> Church

"Max's powerful Pocket Prayer will help you become more mindful of God throughout your day. Experience the inspiration of vintage Lucado—the preacher-poet at his storytelling best."

> — Ken Shigematsu,
> pastor, Tenth Church
> Vancouver; and best-
> selling author, *God in My
> Everything*

"Max Lucado has always been able to boil spiritual truth down to its most potent form. Jesus exhibited faith in constant connection with his Father. This powerful but simple treatise will help you follow in the prayer-steps of the Savior."

> — Chris Fabry, author,
> *Every Waking Moment*;
> and host, Chris Fabry
> Live! on Moody Radio

"*Before Amen* had hand grenade impact on me. Spirit, soul, and body. How do we 'pray without ceasing'? *Before Amen* is revelatory frag that tore through my ignorance concerning 1 Thessalonians 5:17. I set my personal best time reading *Before Amen*. Three hours that has exploded my understanding of prayer forever!"

> — Matthew Crouch, Trinity
> Broadcasting Family of
> Network

"When I read Max he makes me smile, and then, of course, tears come too. This book on prayer is full of Lucado wit, wisdom, and humility. His Pocket Prayer is a gem."

— Dave Toycen, president
and CEO, World Vision
Canada

"If you struggle to pray, to find the right words or enough time, then this book will be a gift to your soul. In a chaotic world Max teaches us how to find rest and strength through prayer."

— Sheila Walsh, author,
The Storm Inside; and
Women of Faith® speaker

"*Amen* is that ageless word that draws a conclusion to our desperate pleas for help or our deep longings for hope. In this book, Max Lucado helps us get a better grip on the words that go before it and the God who listens to them. *Before Amen* is a winsome look at the power generated through the humble, unvarnished prayers we offer to our gracious God."

— Dr. Tim Kimmel, author,
Grace Filled Marriage

"This era of 'always-on' information can feel assaulting and overwhelming. We don't need more complexity. We need simplicity, clarity, and encouragement. We need tools to calm our minds and direct our lives toward Christ. That's what Max Lucado brings through his warm and insightful book on the power of simple prayer. He gives us something precious: the good news that praying powerfully is attainable for all of us. Read it often. Pray it daily. Live it always."

— Bruxy Cavey, best-selling
author, *End of Religion*;
and teaching pastor, The
Meeting House

"Being the new adoptive mama of a very active five-year-old girl, I feel like I'm constantly playing catch up, not to mention being a tad sleep deprived! So it was with great joy and a deep soul sigh that I read *Before Amen* about the power of simple prayer. Sometimes just knowing Jesus loves us enough to lean in and listen when we ask him for help is enough. Max reminded me of that in a way I won't soon forget . . . I loved this book."

— Lisa Harper, Bible
teacher, author, and
Women of Faith® speaker

"Max Lucado's newest project is a must read especially for people like me who struggle with prayer. *Before Amen* not only encourages the heart, it emboldens the soul. Lucado's books are masterpieces that give the reader a realistic look at life that will warm your heart and draw you closer to the One who hears our prayers."

— Wayne Cordeiro, founder
and senior pastor, New
Hope Oahu Church

before
amen

ALSO BY MAX LUCADO

before
amen

The Power of a Simple Prayer

MAX LUCADO

THOMAS NELSON
Since 1798

NASHVILLE   MEXICO CITY   RIO DE JANEIRO

Published in Nashville, Tennessee, by Thomas Nelson. Thomas Nelson is a registered trademark of HarperCollins Christian Publishing, Inc.

Thomas Nelson titles may be purchased in bulk for educational, business, fundraising, or sales promotional use. For information, please e-mail SpecialMarkets@ ThomasNelson.com.

Unless otherwise noted, Scripture quotations are taken from THE NEW KING JAMES VERSION®. © 1982 by Thomas Nelson. Used by permission. All rights reserved.

Other Scripture references are from the following sources: THE ENGLISH STANDARD VERSION © 2001 by Crossway Bibles, a division of Good News Publishers (ESV). God's Word (GOD'S WORD) is a copyrighted work of God's Word to the Nations Bible Society. Quotations are used by permission. © 1995 by God's Word to the Nations Bible Society. All rights reserved. Holman Christian Standard Bible (HCSB). © 1999, 2000, 2002, 2003, 2009 by Broadman and Holman Publishers. All rights reserved. *The Message* (MSG) by Eugene H. Peterson. © 1993, 1994, 1995, 1996, 2000, 2001, 2002. Used by permission of NavPress Publishing Group. All rights reserved. New American Standard Bible® (NASB). © The Lockman Foundation 1960, 1962, 1963, 1968, 1971, 1972, 1973, 1975, 1977, 1995. Used by permission. New Century Version® (NCV). © 2005 by Thomas Nelson, Inc. Used by permission. All rights reserved. Holy Bible, New International Version®, NIV® (NIV). © 1973, 1978, 1984, 2011 by Biblica, Inc.™ Used by permission of Zondervan. All rights reserved worldwide. www.zondervan.com. *Holy Bible*, New Living Translation (NLT). © 1996, 2004, 2007. Used by permission of Tyndale House Publishers, Inc., Wheaton, Illinois 60189. All rights reserved. NEW REVISED STANDARD VERSION of the Bible (NRSV). © 1989 by the Division of Christian Education of the National Council of the Churches of Christ in the U.S.A. All rights reserved. *The Living Bible* (TLB). © 1971. Used by permission of Tyndale House Publishers, Inc., Wheaton, Illinois 60189. All rights reserved.

ISBN 978-0-7180-3283-8 (SE)
ISBN 978-0-7180-1637-1 (IE)

Library of Congress Cataloging-in-Publication Data

Lucado, Max.
  Before amen : the power of a simple prayer / Max Lucado.
    pages cm
  Includes bibliographical references.
  ISBN 978-0-8499-4848-0
  1. Prayer—Christianity. I. Title.
  BV210.3.L825 2014
  248.3'2—dc23   2014007855

Printed in the United States of America

14 15 16 17 18 RRD 6 5 4 3 2 1

To Mark Tidwell,

dear friend,

able coworker,

soldier in the faith

He does what's best for those who fear him—
hears them call out, and saves them.

Psalm 145:19 MSG

Contents

Contents

Acknowledgments

My longtime editors, Liz Heaney and Karen Hill. You are Michelangelo on a manuscript. You keep chiseling until something emerges that is worth seeing. Thank you for pounding away.

The publishing team of David Moberg, Paula Major, Liz Johnson, LeeEric Fesko, Greg and Susan Ligon, Jana Muntsinger, and Pamela McClure. You are ever energetic, accessible, creative, and passionate.

Steve and Cheryl Green. You captain countless projects and comfort dozens of people. You solve problems like superheroes. I don't know what I did to deserve friends like you, but I would do it again.

Carol Bartley, copy editor. We all feel better knowing this: Carol will make sure it is done correctly. So grateful for your diligence.

Randy and Rozanne Frazee. Steady, sturdy, and strong. What an honor to work with you.

The Oak Hills Church. After a quarter of a century, we are still growing together.

Special appreciation to Tina Chisholm, Margaret Mechinus, Janie Padilla, and Ashley Rosales. You serve quietly and graciously, and you deserve far more applause than you receive. Thank you.

David Drury. Ever available to disentangle knots and thoughts and to offer advice.

David Treat. Always prayerful, always praying.

My daughters and son-in-law: Andrea, Sara, Jenna, Brett. When I look at you, I know the meaning of *blessing*.

And Denalyn, my dear wife. My favorite answered prayer? *Lord, let her say yes.* He did. You placed the ring on your finger and took your place in my heart . . . forever.

one

The Pocket Prayer

Hello, my name is Max. I'm a recovering prayer wimp. I doze off when I pray. My thoughts zig, then zag, then zig again. Distractions swarm like gnats on a summer night. If attention deficit disorder applies to prayer, I am afflicted. When I pray, I think of a thousand things I need to do. I forget the one thing I set out to do: pray.

Some people excel in prayer. They inhale heaven and exhale God. They are the SEAL Team Six of intercession. They would rather pray than sleep. Why is it that I sleep when I pray? They belong to the PGA: Prayer Giants Association. I am a card-carrying member of the PWA: Prayer Wimps Anonymous.

Can you relate? It's not that we don't pray at all. We all pray some.

On tearstained pillows we pray.

In grand liturgies we pray.

At the sight of geese in flight, we pray.

Quoting ancient devotions, we pray.

This week more of us will pray than will exercise, go to work, or have sex.[1] Surveys indicate that one in five unbelievers prays daily.[2] Just in case?

We pray to stay sober, centered, or solvent. We pray when the lump is deemed malignant. When the money runs out before the month does. When the unborn baby hasn't kicked in a while. We all pray . . . some.

But wouldn't we all like to pray . . .

More?

Better?

Deeper?

Stronger?

With more fire, faith, or fervency?

Yet we have kids to feed, bills to pay, deadlines to meet. The calendar pounces on our good intentions like a tiger on a rabbit. We want to pray, but *when*?

We want to pray, but *why*? We might as well admit it. Prayer is odd, peculiar. Speaking into space. Lifting words into the sky. We can't even get the cable company to answer us, yet God will? The doctor is too busy, but God isn't? We have our doubts about prayer.

And we have our checkered history with prayer: unmet expectations, unanswered requests. We can barely genuflect for the scar tissue on our knees. God, to some, is the ultimate heartbreaker. Why keep tossing the coins of our longings into a silent pool? He jilted me once . . . but not twice.

Oh, the peculiar puzzle of prayer.

We aren't the first to struggle. The sign-up sheet for Prayer 101 contains some familiar names: the apostles John, James, Andrew, and Peter. When one of Jesus' disciples requested, "Lord, teach us to pray" (Luke 11:1 NIV), none of the others objected. No one walked away saying, "Hey, I have prayer figured out." The first followers of Jesus needed prayer guidance.

> The first followers of Jesus needed prayer guidance. In fact, the only tutorial they ever requested was on prayer.

In fact, the only tutorial they ever requested was on prayer. They could have asked for instructions on many topics: bread multiplying, speech making, storm stilling. Jesus raised people from the dead. But a "How to Vacate the Cemetery" seminar? His followers never called for one. But they did want him to do this: "Lord, teach us to pray."

Might their interest have had something to do with the jaw-dropping, eye-popping promises Jesus attached to prayer? "Ask and it will be given to you" (Matt. 7:7 NIV). "If you believe, you will get anything you ask for in prayer" (Matt. 21:22 NCV). Jesus never attached such power to other endeavors. "*Plan* and it will be given to you." "You will get anything you *work* for." Those words are not in the Bible. But these are—"If you remain in me and follow my teachings, you can ask anything you want, and it will be given to you" (John 15:7 NCV).

Jesus gave stunning prayer promises.

And he set a compelling prayer example. Jesus prayed before he ate. He prayed for children. He prayed for the sick. He prayed with thanks. He prayed with tears. He had made the planets and shaped the stars, yet he prayed. He is the Lord of angels and Commander of heavenly hosts, yet he prayed. He is coequal with God, the exact representation of the Holy One, and yet he devoted himself to prayer. He prayed in the desert, cemetery, and garden. "He went out and departed to a solitary place; and there He prayed" (Mark 1:35).

This dialogue must have been common among his friends:

"Has anyone seen Jesus?"

"Oh, you know. He's up to the same thing."

"Praying *again*?

"Yep. He's been gone since sunrise."

Jesus would even disappear for an entire night of prayer. I'm thinking of one occasion in particular. He'd just experienced one of the most stressful days of his ministry. The day began with the news of the death of his relative John the Baptist. Jesus sought to retreat with his disciples, yet a throng of thousands followed him. Though grief-stricken, he spent the day teaching and healing people. When it was discovered that the host of people had no food to eat, Jesus multiplied bread out of a basket and fed the entire multitude. In the span of a few hours, he battled sorrow, stress, demands, and needs. He deserved a good night's rest. Yet when evening finally came, he told the crowd to leave and the disciples to board their boat, and "he went up into the hills by himself to pray" (Mark 6:46 NLT).

Apparently it was the correct choice. A storm exploded over the Sea of Galilee, leaving the disciples "in trouble far away from land, for a strong wind had risen, and they were fighting heavy waves. About three o'clock in the morning Jesus came toward them, walking on the water" (Matt. 14:24–25 NLT). Jesus ascended the mountain depleted. He reappeared invigorated. When he reached the water, he never broke his stride. You'd have thought the water was a park lawn and the storm a spring breeze.

Do you think the disciples made the prayer–power connection? "Lord, teach us to pray *like that*. Teach us to find strength in prayer. To banish fear in prayer. To defy storms in prayer. To come off the mountain of prayer with the authority of a prince."

> When the disciples asked Jesus to teach them to pray, he gave them a prayer. Not a lecture on prayer. Not the doctrine of prayer. He gave them a quotable, repeatable, portable prayer.

What about you? The disciples faced angry waves and a watery grave. You face angry clients, a turbulent economy, raging seas of stress and sorrow.

"Lord," we still request, "teach us to pray."

When the disciples asked Jesus to teach them to pray, he gave them a prayer. Not a lecture on prayer. Not the doctrine of prayer. He gave them a quotable, repeatable, portable prayer (Luke 11:1–4).

Could you use the same? It seems to me that the

prayers of the Bible can be distilled into one. The result is a simple, easy-to-remember, pocket-size prayer:

Father,

> *you are good.*

> > *I need help. Heal me and forgive me.*

> > *They need help.*

> > *Thank you.*

> > *In Jesus' name, amen.*

Let this prayer punctuate your day. As you begin your morning, *Father, you are good.* As you commute to work or walk the hallways at school, *I need help.* As you wait in the grocery line, *They need help.* Keep this prayer in your pocket as you pass through the day.

Prayer, for most of us, is not a matter of a month-long retreat or even an hour of meditation. Prayer is conversation with God while driving to work or awaiting an appointment or before interacting with a client. Prayer can be the internal voice that directs the external action.

> Prayer is conversation with God while driving to work or awaiting an appointment or before interacting with a client.

This much is sure: God will teach you to pray.

Don't think for a minute that he is glaring at you from a distance with crossed arms and a scowl, waiting for

> This much is sure: God will teach you to pray.

you to get your prayer life together. Just the opposite. "Here I am! I stand at the door and knock. If you hear my voice and open the door, I will come in and eat with you, and you will eat with me" (Rev. 3:20 NCV).

Jesus waits on the porch. He stands on the threshold. He taps . . . and calls. He waits for you to open the door. To pray is to open it. Prayer is the hand of faith on the door handle of your heart. The willing pull. The happy welcome to Jesus: "Come in, O King. Come in." "The kitchen is messy, but come in." "I didn't clean up, but come in." "I'm not much of a conversationalist, but come in."

We speak. He listens. He speaks. We listen. This is prayer in its purest form. God changes his people through such moments.

He is changing me! Yes, I am a prayer wimp, but a *recovering* prayer wimp. Not where I long to be, but not where I was. My time in prayer has become my time of power. The Pocket Prayer has become a cherished friend. Its phrases linger in my thoughts like a favorite melody.

Father,
> *you are good.*
>> *I need help. Heal me and forgive me.*
>> *They need help.*
>> *Thank you.*
>>> *In Jesus' name, amen.*

When we invite God into our world, he walks in. He brings a host of gifts: joy, patience, resilience. Anxieties come, but they don't stick. Fears surface and then depart. Regrets land on the windshield, but then comes the wiper of prayer. The devil still hands me stones of guilt, but I turn and give them to Christ. I'm completing my sixth decade, yet I'm wired with energy. I am happier, healthier, and more hopeful than I have ever been. Struggles come, for sure. But so does God.

Prayer is not a privilege for the pious, not the art of a chosen few. Prayer is simply

> We speak. He listens. He speaks. We listen. This is prayer in its purest form. God changes his people through such moments.

a heartfelt conversation between God and his child. My friend, he wants to talk with you. Even now, as you read these words, he taps at the door. Open it. Welcome him in. Let the conversation begin.

two

Father . . . Daddy

When my eldest daughter was thirteen years old, she flubbed her piano piece at a recital. Jenna went on to become a fine pianist and a wonderful singer. But everyone has an off day. She just happened to have hers in front of an auditorium crowded with family, friends, and onlookers. The performance started well. Her fingers flowed up and down the keyboard like Billy Joel's. But midway through the piece, her musical train jumped the track.

I can still see her staring straight ahead, fingers stuck as if in superglue. She backed up a few measures and took another run at it. No luck. For the life of her she couldn't remember the next part. The silence in the auditorium was broken only by the pounding of her parents' hearts.

Come on, honey, you can do it.

Keep trying.

Don't give up. It will come.

Finally it did. Jenna's mental block broke, and she completed the piece. But the damage had been done. She stood up from the piano bench, chin quivering, and curtsied. The audience offered compassionate applause. She hurried off the stage. Denalyn and I scurried out of our seats and met her at the side of the auditorium. She threw her arms around me and buried her face in my shirt.

"Oh, Daddy."

That was enough for me. Denalyn and I sandwiched her with affection. If a hug could extract embarrassment, that one would have. At that moment I would have given her the moon. All she said was, "Oh, Daddy."

> Prayer begins with an honest, heartfelt "Oh, Daddy."

Prayer starts here. Prayer begins with an honest, heartfelt "Oh, Daddy."

Jesus taught us to begin our prayers by saying, "Our

Father in heaven" (Matt. 6:9). More specifically, our "*Abba*
in heaven." *Abba* is an intimate, tender, folksy, pedestrian
term, the warmest of the Aramaic words for "father."[1]

Formality stripped away.
Proximity promised. Jesus
invites us to approach God
the way a child approaches
his or her daddy.

> Jesus invites us
> to approach God
> the way a child
> approaches his
> or her daddy.

And how do children
approach their daddies? I
went to a school playground
to find out. I found a spot on the bench under the awning,
flipped open a notebook, and took notes. Most of the
children were picked up by their mothers. Yet enough
dads had car-pool duty for me to complete my research.
When a five-year-old spots his father in the parking lot,
how does he react?

"Yippee!" (screamed by a redheaded boy wearing a
Batman backpack).

"Ice cream!" (apparently referring to a promise made
by the fellow to the freckle-faced girl).

"Pop! Over here! Push me!" (yelled by a boy wearing a Boston Red Sox cap who scooted straight to the
swings).

I heard requests: "Daddy, can Tommy come home

with me? His mom is on a business trip, and he doesn't want to hang out with his big sister because she won't let him watch TV and makes him eat . . . " (The boy's mouth was an uncapped hydrant. The words never stopped.)

I heard questions: "Are we going home?" And I heard excitement: "Daddy! Look what I did!"

Here's what I didn't hear: "Father, it is most gracious of thee to drive thy car to my place of education and provide me with domestic transportation. Please know of my deep gratitude for your benevolence. For thou art splendid in thy attentive care and diligent in thy dedication."

I didn't hear formality or impressive vocabulary. I heard kids who were happy to see their dads and eager to speak.

God invites us to approach him in the same manner. What a relief! We prayer wimps fear "mis-praying." What are the expected etiquette and dress code of prayer? What if we kneel instead of stand? What if we say the wrong words or use the wrong tone? Am I apostate if I say "prostate" instead of "prostrate"?

Jesus' answer? "Unless you are converted and become as little children, you will by no means enter the kingdom of heaven" (Matt. 18:3). *Become as little children.*

Carefree. Joy filled. Playful. Trusting. Curious. Excited. Forget greatness; seek littleness. Trust more; strut less. Make lots of requests, and accept all the gifts. Come to God the way a child comes to Daddy.

Daddy. The term takes aim at our pride. Other salutations permit an air of sophistication. As a pastor I know this well. Deepen the tone of voice, and pause for dramatic effect. "O holy Lord . . . " I allow the words to reverberate throughout the universe as I, the pontiff of petition, pontificate my prayer.

> Forget greatness; seek littleness. Trust more; strut less. Make lots of requests, and accept all the gifts. Come to God the way a child comes to Daddy.

"God, you are my King, and I am your prince."

"God, you are the Maestro, and I am your minstrel."

"God, you are the President, and I am your ambassador."

But God prefers this greeting: "God, you are my Daddy, and I am your child."

Here's why: it's hard to show off and call God "Daddy" at the same time. Impossible, in fact. Perhaps this is the point. Elsewhere, Jesus gives this instruction: "When you pray, don't be like the hypocrites. They love to stand in the synagogues and on the street corners and pray so people will see them. I tell you the truth, they already have their full reward" (Matt. 6:5 NCV).

> It's hard to show off and call God "Daddy" at the same time. Impossible, in fact. Perhaps this is the point.

Religious leaders loved (and still love) to make theater out of their prayers. They perched themselves at intersections and practiced public piety. The show nauseated Jesus. "When you pray, you should go into your room and close the door and pray to your Father who cannot be seen. Your Father can see what is done in secret, and he will reward you" (Matt. 6:6 NCV).

The words surely stunned Jesus' audience. Prayer, they likely assumed, was reserved for special people in a special place. God met with the priest in the temple, behind the curtain, in the Holy of Holies. The people were simple farmers and stonemasons. Folks of the land and earth. They couldn't enter the temple. But they could enter their closets.

"Go into your room and close the door . . . " In the

Palestinian culture the room most likely to have a door was the storage closet. It held tools, seed, and farming supplies. A chicken might even wander in. There was nothing holy in it. Nothing holy about it. It was the day-to-day workroom.[2]

It still is. My closet has no fancy fixtures or impressive furniture. It has a shoe rack, a dirty-clothes hamper, hangers, and drawers for socks and underwear.

I don't entertain guests in my closet. You'll never hear me tell visitors after dinner, "Why don't we step into the closet for a chat?" Denalyn and I prefer the living room or the den. God apparently likes to chat in the closet.

The point? He's low on fancy, high on accessibility. To pray at the Vatican can be meaningful. But prayers offered at home carry as much weight as prayers offered in Rome. Travel to the Wailing Wall if you want. But prayer at your backyard fence is just as effective. The One who hears your prayers is your Daddy. You needn't woo him with location.

> God apparently likes to chat in the closet. The point? He's low on fancy, high on accessibility.

Or wow him with eloquence. Jesus continued, "And

when you pray, don't be like those people who don't know God. They continue saying things that mean nothing, thinking that God will hear them because of their many words. Don't be like them, because your Father knows the things you need before you ask him" (Matt. 6:7–8 NCV).

Jesus downplayed the importance of words in prayers. We tend to do the opposite. The more words the better. The *better* words the better. Muslim prayers, however impressive, must be properly recited at each of the five appointed times during the day. Hindu and Buddhist prayers, however profound, depend upon the repetition of mantras, words, and syllables. Even branches of the Christian faith emphasize the appropriate prayer language, the latest prayer trend, the holiest prayer terminology. Against all this emphasis on syllables and rituals, Jesus says, "Don't ramble like heathens who . . . talk a lot" (Matt. 6:7 GOD'S WORD).

> Just as a happy child cannot mis-hug, the sincere heart cannot mis-pray.

Vocabulary and geography might impress people but not God. There is no panel of angelic judges with numbered cards. "Wow, Lucado, that prayer was a ten.

God will certainly hear you!" "Oh, Lucado, you scored a two this morning. Go home and practice." Prayers aren't graded according to style.

Just as a happy child cannot mis-hug, the sincere heart cannot mis-pray. Heaven knows, life has enough burdens without the burden of praying correctly. If prayer depends on how I pray, I'm sunk. But if the power of prayer depends on the One who hears the prayer, and if the One who hears the prayer is my Daddy, then I have hope.

> If prayer depends on how I pray, I'm sunk. But if the power of prayer depends on the One who hears the prayer, and if the One who hears the prayer is my Daddy, then I have hope.

Prayer really is that simple. Resist the urge to complicate it. Don't take pride in well-crafted prayers. Don't apologize for incoherent prayers. No games. No cover-ups. Just be honest—honest to God. Climb into his lap. Tell him everything that is on your heart. Or tell him nothing at all. Just lift your heart to heaven and declare, *Father . . . Daddy . . .*

And sometimes "Daddy" is all we can muster. Stress.

Fear. Guilt. Grief. Demands on all sides. All we can summon is a plaintive "Oh, Father." If so, that's enough. It was for my young daughter. Jenna uttered only two words, and I wrapped her in my arms. Your heavenly Father will do the same.

three

You Are Good

As I boarded a plane last week, the pilot called my name. He was standing in the cockpit entrance, greeting passengers. "Well, hello, Max." I looked up. It was my friend Joe. My *old* friend. He is the Methuselah of the airways. He's been flying forever. He flew transports in Vietnam and has logged a bookful of hours as a commercial pilot. He's faced every flight crisis from electrical storms to empty fuel tanks. He is a good pilot.

And he is a friend, a *good* friend. He's not my neighbor, but if he were, our property value would increase. If I were in the hospital, he'd keep a bedside vigil. If I were on vacation, he'd keep my dog. If I offended him, he'd keep his cool until we could talk it through. He could no more tell a lie than a mosquito could sing the national anthem. He never swears, gets drunk, cheats, or swindles. He is that good.

He is good—good in skill and good in heart.

We chatted for a few minutes, and I went to my seat with a sense of assurance. *What more could I request?* I thought. *The pilot is experienced and proven. Even more, he is my tried-and-true friend. I am in good hands.*

The knowledge came in handy. An hour into the flight we hit a wall of winds. People gasped, dentures rattled, and the attendant told us to check our seat belts and rosary beads. I've had smoother roller coaster rides. Unlike the other passengers, however, I stayed calm. I didn't have a death wish, but I had an advantage. I knew the pilot. I knew Joe. I knew his heart and trusted his skill. *Joe can handle this*, I told myself. The storm was bad, but the pilot was good. So as much as one can relax in a squall, I did.

Friend, it's a stormy world out there. Every day brings turbulence. Moody economy. Aging bodies. Declining job market. Increasing street violence. The question during these troubling times is this: Do we have a good pilot?

The resounding response of the Bible is yes!

You are good, LORD. (Ps. 25:7 NCV)

Good and upright is the LORD. (Ps. 25:8 NIV)

You, Lord, are forgiving and good. (Ps. 86:5 NIV)

God is good—good in skill and good in heart.

Most people suffer from small thoughts about God. In an effort to see him as our friend, we have lost his immensity. In our desire to understand him, we have sought to contain him. The God of the Bible cannot be contained. He brought order out of chaos and created creation. With a word he called Adam out of dust and Eve out of a bone. He consulted no committee. He sought no counsel.

He has no peer. "I am God, and there is no other; I am God, and there is none like me" (Isa. 46:9 NIV). The greatest kings have surrendered their crowns. Alexander the Great is a mound of dust in a tomb. The queen of England is called Her Majesty, yet she must eat and bathe and rest. The True Majesty, on the other hand, is never hungry. He never sleeps. He has never needed attention or assistance.

From the tiniest microbe to the mightiest mountain, "he sustains everything by the mighty power of his command" (Heb. 1:3 NLT).

He has authority over the world and . . .

He has authority over *your* world. Your sleep patterns.

Your eating habits. Your salary. The traffic of your commute. The arthritis in your joints. God reigns over all these. He's never surprised. He has never, ever uttered the phrase "How did that happen?"

God's power is unsurpassed.

And his heart is unblemished. "There is nothing deceitful in God, nothing two-faced, nothing fickle" (James 1:17 MSG). He has no hidden agenda or selfish motive. He loves with a good love and forgives with a good forgiveness. *Good* as in "beautiful, best . . . bountiful."[1]

> If God were only mighty, we would salute him. But since he is merciful and mighty, we can approach him.

God's goodness is a major headline in the Bible. I think I know why. If God were only mighty, we would salute him. But since he is merciful and mighty, we can approach him. No wonder the psalmist invited, "Taste and see that the LORD is good" (Ps. 34:8 NLT). A glimpse of God's goodness changes us.

God's unrivaled goodness undergirds everything else we can say about prayer. If he is like us, only slightly stronger, then why pray? If he grows weary, then why pray? If he has limitations, questions, and hesitations, then you might as well pray to the Wizard of Oz.

However, if God is at once Father and Creator, holy—unlike us—and high above us, then we at any point are only a prayer away from help.

When I was fifteen years old, I inherited a Rambler station wagon from my big brother. Look up the word *jalopy* in the dictionary, and you might see a picture of the car. Faded paint, standard shift on the column, worn interior. It wasn't much to look at, but it was mine.

> If God is at once Father and Creator, holy—unlike us—and high above us, then we at any point are only a prayer away from help.

My brother was heading off to college in his graduation present, a used Plymouth. And I was entrusted with the Rambler. I remember the passing of the keys.

"You have to keep gas in the tank," Dad advised.

"I know."

"Air in the tires."

"I know."

"Can you change the oil and keep the car washed?"

"Of course I can," I lied. Truth be told, I didn't know

the difference between a manifold and a windshield wiper. Which was odd since my dad was a mechanic. He made a living repairing oil field engines. And he made a hobby out of rebuilding car engines. He worked with machines like Monet worked with colors—daily and delightfully. He tried to teach me the trade, and I tried to learn, but when it came to machines, my brain was Teflon. Nothing stuck.

I wasn't about to tell that to my father though.

My ineptness surfaced the following Saturday. Dad reminded me that it was time to change the oil in the Rambler.

"Do you know how to do it?"

"Yes," I answered.

"You want me to help you?"

I should have said yes.

I spent an hour beneath the car looking for the oil pan and another hour wrestling with the plug. I finally removed it, drained the oil, crawled out, and poured in five new quarts. Finished at last.

Or so I thought. Dad was waiting for me in the garage.

"All done?"

"All done."

"You sure?"

"Yessir."

"Then what is that?"

He pointed to a river of oil running down the driveway—clean oil. I'd forgotten to replace the plug in the oil pan.

"Max," he said, "we need to talk." He walked me over to his oil field pickup. He opened the side panel and showed me the trays of tools. He began to describe the purpose of each. "I use this one to remove valves, this one to tighten clamps, this one to attach hoses, this one to . . . "

He took me tool by tool through his truck. After what seemed like an hour of show-and-tell, he closed the cabinet, locked it, and looked me straight in the eye. "Son," he said, "I fix things for a living. What is hard for you is simple to me. I may not be good at everything, but I am good with machines. Let me help you. I'm a mechanic. And, besides, I'm your dad."

I never spilled another drop of oil. (Of course, now I pay the guy at the lube store to do the work.)

Here is what I think: our toughest challenges are simple oil changes to God.

Here is what else I think: a lot of us make unnecessary messes.

But we can change that.

May I make a suggestion? Before you face the world, face your Father.

> Before you face the world, face your Father.

Here is how it works. It's a Monday morning. The alarm clock lives up to its name. *Clang! Clang! Clang!* You groan, roll over, and sit up. In the old days you would have made the coffee, turned on the news, and begun your day with a briefing on the toxic problems in the world.

But today you turn to the Pocket Prayer. Still half asleep you take your coffee, and you lumber toward a chair and take a seat. You don't look like much: face pillow creased, hair smashed. No matter. You haven't come to look at you. You have come to look at God.

Father, my Daddy . . . The words come slowly at first. But you stay at it. *You are good. Your heart is good. Your ways are right* . . . The words stir you. Something within begins to awaken. *The weather is bad, the economy is bad, but, God, you are awesome.*

Don't underestimate the power of this moment. You just opened the door to God and welcomed truth to enter your heart. Faith sneaked in while despair was dozing.

Who knows, you might start to worship.

Father, you are good. Good enough to love me, care for me, and come for me. You are good! An arch of your eyebrow, and a million angels will pivot and salute. Every throne is a footstool to yours. Every crown is papier-mâché to yours. You have no questions, second thoughts, or backward glances. You consult no clock. You keep no calendar. You report to no one. You are good!

Is your world different because you prayed? In one sense, no. Wars still rage, traffic still clogs, and heartbreakers still roam the planet. But you are different. You have peace. You've spent time with the Pilot. And the Pilot is up to the task.

My friend Joe, as it turns out, got us through the storm just fine. He landed the plane and stood in his cockpit door as we exited the flight.

"Got a bit choppy there, Joe," I commented.

"Yeah," he agreed. "Were you scared?"

"Not really," I replied. "Everything changes when you know the pilot."

four

I Need Help

Do you want to see a father's face go ashen? Do you want to hear a mother gasp? Then position yourself nearby as they discover these three words on the box of a just-bought toy: "Some assembly required."

What the parents wanted was a gift for their child. What they got was a project—sometimes a project for life. They moan, groan, and wonder if it is worth it. They retrieve the minimal tools: a screwdriver, a hammer, and a welding truck. What follows are several late-night hours of squeezing A into B, bolting D into F, sliding R over Z, and hoping no one notices if steps four, five, and six were skipped altogether.

I'm convinced the devil indwells the details of toy assembly. Hell releases tiny minions into the work station of the unsuspecting parent so the little devils can scamper off with brackets, bolts, and screws. Somewhere in perdition is a warehouse of stolen toy parts.

"Some assembly required." Not the most welcome sentence but an honest one. Marriage licenses should include the words "Some assembly required" in large print. Job contracts should state in bold letters "Some assembly required." Babies should exit the womb with a toe tag: "Some assembly required."

Life is a gift, albeit unassembled. It comes in pieces, and sometimes it falls to pieces. Part A doesn't always fit with part B. The struggle is too great for the strength. Inevitably, something seems to be missing. The pieces of life don't fit. When they don't, take your problem to Jesus.

Mary, the mother of Jesus, did. "On the third day there was a wedding in Cana of Galilee, and the mother of Jesus was there. Now both Jesus and His disciples were invited to the wedding" (John 2:1–2).

A common wedding. The bride wasn't the daughter of an emperor. The groom wasn't a prince. Were it not for one detail, the event would've been lost in time. The guest list. It read something like this:

Benjamin of Capernaum
Simon the craftsman
Saul, rabbi of Cana

And farther down the list:

Jesus of Nazareth

The family invited Jesus to a wedding. Since he always goes where he is invited, Jesus and his disciples traveled to Cana for their first excursion. While they were there, the wedding party "ran out of wine" (v. 3). Someone underestimated the size of the crowd or the appetite of the guests or the depth of the wine vats or the number of friends Jesus would bring. As a result the bride and groom ran out of wine. In your case the department ran out of cash, the team ran out of solutions, or you've run out of energy. Life leaks.

Enter, stage right, Mary, the mother of Jesus. For my nickel she appears too seldom in Scripture. After all, who knew Jesus better than she did? She carried him for nine months. Breast-fed him for more. She heard his first words and witnessed his first steps. She was the ultimate authority on Jesus. So on the rare occasion she speaks, we perk up. "The mother of Jesus said to Him, 'They have no wine'" (v. 3).

Mary wasn't bossy. She didn't say, "Jesus, they are out of wine, so here is what I need you to do. Go down to the grove at the corner, accelerate the growth of some Bordeaux grapes, and turn them into wine." She didn't try to fix the problem herself.

She wasn't critical. "If only they had planned better, Jesus. People just don't think ahead. What is society coming to? The world is going over the cliff! Help, Jesus, help!" She didn't blame the host.

She didn't blame Jesus. "What kind of Messiah are you? If you truly were in control, this never would have happened!"

Nor did she blame herself. "It's all my fault, Jesus. Punish me. I failed as a friend. Now the wedding is ruined. The marriage will collapse. I am to blame."

None of this. Mary didn't whine about the wine. She just stated the problem.

Then "Jesus said to her, 'Woman, what does your concern have to do with Me? My hour has not yet come.' His mother said to the servants, 'Whatever He says to you, do it'" (vv. 4–5).

Originally, Jesus had no intention of saving the wedding banquet. This wasn't the manner or place he had planned to reveal his power. But then Mary entered the story—Mary, someone he loved—with a genuine need.

In my imagination I see Mary turn and walk away. Her face is serene. Her eyes reflect calm. She is untroubled. She has done everything she was supposed to do. She has identified the problem, brought it to Jesus, and left it with him. She trusted him completely. She told the servants, "Whatever he says is okay with me."

In my imagination I see Jesus smile. I hear him chuckle. He looks up into the heavens for a moment and then looks at a cluster of six waterpots over in the corner.

> Jesus said to them [the servants], "Fill the waterpots with water." And they filled them up to the brim. And He said to them, "Draw some out now, and take it to the master of the feast." (vv. 7–8)

The master of the feast tasted the wine and licked his lips and said, "This is good stuff!" Then he lifted his glass in a toast to the bridegroom and complimented him for saving the best wine until last.

While the master of the feast noted the quality of the wine, John wanted us to observe the quantity. Six stone jars capable of holding thirty gallons apiece. The servants filled them to the brim (v. 7). At Jesus' command H2O became abundant merlot. Quick calculation reveals the amount: 908 bottles of wine![1] The couple could have begun a wine business in Napa Valley.

Problem presented. Prayer answered. Crisis avoided. All because Mary entrusted the problem to Jesus.

There is another version of this story. In it Mary never involved Jesus. She took the master of the feast to task for poor planning. He took exception to her accusations. Mary stormed out of the party. The groom overheard the argument and lost his temper. The bride told her groom to forget marriage. If he couldn't manage his anger, he sure couldn't manage a home. By the end of the day, the guests left sad, the marriage was ended before it began, and Jesus shook his head and said, "I could've helped if only I'd been asked."

> How many disasters would be averted if we'd go first, in faith, to Jesus?

That version of the story isn't in the Bible, but the principle surely exists in life. We can only wonder: How many disasters would be averted if we'd go first, in faith, to Jesus?

The punch line is clear: *take your problem to Jesus.* Don't take your problems to the bar. Jim Beam cannot solve them. Don't take your problems out on others.

Temper tantrums never advance the cause. The moment you sense a problem, however large or small, take it to Christ.

"Max, if I take my problems to Jesus every time I have one, I am going to be talking to Jesus all day long." (Now you are getting the point.)

> Don't worry about anything; instead, pray about everything; tell God your needs and don't forget to thank him for his answers. If you do this, you will experience God's peace, which is far more wonderful than the human mind can understand. His peace will keep your thoughts and your hearts quiet and at rest as you trust in Christ Jesus. (Phil. 4:6–7 TLB)

An unprayed-for problem is an embedded thorn. It festers and infects—first the finger, then the hand, then the entire arm. Best to go straight to the person who has the tweezers.

Can I share a time I did this? Two of our three daughters were born in Brazil. Soon after we brought Jenna home from the hospital, we received a surprise. A hefty hospital bill. Our stateside insurance company wouldn't pay the medical charges. To this day I've never understood the issue. No matter how much I pleaded, explained, or cajoled, the insurance company said, "We won't pay." The hospital meanwhile said, "You must pay."

The bill was for $2,500. I checked our account. We had a grand total of $2,500. Good news: we paid the bill. Bad news: we were broke as a result.

During that season of my life, I was learning much about trust. Several verses had become theme promises to me, among them "Be anxious for nothing, but in everything by prayer and supplication, with thanksgiving, let your requests be made known to God" (Phil. 4:6).

I was a novice to anxiety-free living, but I resolved to try. I treated each anxious thought—and there were many—with prayer. *Lord, with your help I will not be anxious. But I am in a foreign country with a new baby and an empty bank account. Hint, hint.*

God took the hint. A speaking invitation came my way. A church flew me to Florida to speak at a retreat. It was the only such opportunity that arose during our five years in Rio de Janeiro. As I was leaving the church to return to the airport, a gentleman handed me an envelope. He wanted to bless the work. Such gifts were common. People often handed us $50 or $75. I thanked him and tucked the envelope into my pocket.

As the plane took off, I opened it. Inside was a check for $2,500! Exactly the amount we needed to replenish what we had lost. That event was a mile-marker moment for me. God keeps his word. I just need to ask.

> God keeps his word. We just need to ask.

What might this look like for you? Imagine this scene. It is breakfast time, and the family is in chaos. The daughters are complaining about their brother who took too much time in the bathroom. As a result their hair isn't brushed and makeup isn't applied. Mom is doing her best to manage the conflict, but she woke up with a headache and a long list of things to do. The clock is ticking like a time bomb, ever closer to that moment when, *boom!* It's time to go. Dad stops at the kitchen entryway and surveys the pandemonium. He weighs his options:

- Command everyone to shape up and behave.
- Berate his son for dominating the bathroom, his daughters for poor planning, and his wife for not taking control.
- Sneak out before anyone notices.

Or he could turn to the Pocket Prayer. *Father, you are good. I need help. Reduce the frenzy in my house, please.* Will the prayer change everything? It may. Or it may take another prayer, or two, or ten. But at least the problem will be in the hands of the One who can solve it. "Cast all your anxiety on him because he cares for you" (1 Peter 5:7 NIV).

Some years ago Pastor Dale Galloway's wife asked him for a divorce. He was left desolate. The days that followed, he said, were "worse than death." In his dark times he offered a prayer: *I need help.*

> I practiced what I call "let go and let God." I took my hands and cupped them in front of me, held them up, and verbally put inside those hands everything I was fretting over and didn't have any answers to. I said out loud as I held up both hands, "There it is, God; I can't change it, I don't know what to do with it, it's all so unacceptable to me. . . I have been fighting it. I just don't know what to do. There it is, Lord, I give it all to you." . . . As I dropped my arms to my side, a wonderful feeling of serenity suddenly spread throughout my entire being. I now had peace in the midst of the storm.[2]

Most of us can take our problems to Christ, but leave them there? For good? With faith? Again, let Mary be our model. She took her problem to Jesus and left it there. "Whatever He says to you, do it." Resist the urge to reclaim the problem once you've given it up.

Helen Roseveare was a missionary doctor who spent twenty years in the Congo at a clinic and orphanage.

> Resist the urge to reclaim the problem once you've given it up.

When Helen had been there almost four years, a mother died in labor, leaving behind a premature baby and a two-year-old girl. The facility had no incubator or electricity. Dr. Roseveare's first task was to keep the newborn warm. She sent a midwife to fetch a hot water bottle. The nurse returned with bad news: the bottle had burst when she filled it. Even worse, that was the last bottle. Dr. Roseveare instructed the midwife to sleep near the newborn. They would seek a solution the next day.

A solution was not easily found. The clinic was in the heart of the jungle. Help was many miles away. The life of the newborn was in jeopardy. The following noon the doctor mentioned the concern to the children. She told them of the frail baby and the sad sister. And they prayed.

A ten-year-old girl named Ruth decided on her own to take the problem to Jesus. "Please, God, send us a hot water bottle. It'll be no good tomorrow, God, as the baby'll be dead; so please send it this afternoon. And, while You are about it, would You please send a dolly for the little girl, so she'll know You really love her?"

The doctor was stunned. That prayer could only be answered by the arrival of a parcel from home. After nearly four years at the clinic, she'd never received a single package. Even if one came, who would send a hot water bottle to the equator?

Someone did. Later that afternoon a twenty-two-pound package was delivered to Helen's door. As she called the children, she felt tears in her eyes. Could it be? They pulled off the string and unwrapped the paper. In the box they found bandages, jerseys, raisins, sultanas, and a brand-new hot water bottle. And at the bottom of the box, a doll for the little girl. The box had been shipped five months earlier. The Lord had heard the prayer before it was even offered.[3]

Pieces don't fit. Wine runs out. Water bottles burst. These are facts of life. But Jesus responds with this invitation: "Bring your problems to me." State them simply. Present them faithfully, and trust him reverently. Odds are you will be raising a glass and proposing a toast before you know it.

five

Heal Me

A daughter of a dying man wrote these words in her journal: "Dad can't tie up his own shoes anymore . . . Dad can't sign his name anymore. Dad breaks his collar bone and stops going to work."

ALS (Lou Gehrig's disease) was claiming her father's muscles. She documented the progress of the disease. "Dad falls in the parking lot and has to wait on the ground until someone picks him up . . . Dad can't have his corn flakes for breakfast anymore. Dad can't put his arms around us anymore . . . Dad has trouble swallowing puréed peas . . . Dad can't hold his head up anymore."

After seven years of her father's deterioration, finally she wrote this: "Lying beside Dad as he sits in his chair working for breath. Praying for peace. Wiping his nose. Rubbing his shoulders . . . Watching Dad gaze heavenward and take his last quiet breath . . . The Lord is our shepherd."

The family selected two Scripture verses for the funeral handout. On one side: "The Lord is my shepherd, and so I lack nothing." Across from it: "My God! My God! . . . Why have you forsaken me?"[1] The first passage is from Psalm 23, and the other, Psalm 22. In my Bible I can see both passages in the same page opening.

In times of sickness we can hear both prayers from the same heart. Our bodies ache and emotions sway. Try as we might to eat right, sleep more, and sweat often, the hounds of wear and tear nip at our heels. Sometimes they take a bite. Cancer, heart failure, depression, dementia. Nothing bends our knees to ask for God's help more than a health crisis. We need the Lord to shepherd us through sickness.

"But will he?" we quietly question. "Will he?" we verbally demand. "My God! My God! . . . Why?" We see good, prayerful people wheelchair bound or disease ridden. We see salt-of-the-earth folks struck down in their prime. We see evildoers live into triple digits. "Have you forsaken me?" How do we explain the *why* and *when* of God's healing?

We might begin in Jericho:

> Now as they went out of Jericho, a great multitude followed Him. And behold, two blind men sitting by the road, when they heard that Jesus was passing by, cried out, saying, "Have mercy on us, O Lord, Son of David!"
>
> Then the multitude warned them that they should be quiet; but they cried out all the more, saying, "Have mercy on us, O Lord, Son of David!"
>
> So Jesus stood still and called them, and said, "What do you want Me to do for you?"
>
> They said to Him, "Lord, that our eyes may be opened." So Jesus had compassion and touched their eyes. And immediately their eyes received sight, and they followed Him. (Matt. 20:29–34)

The popularity of Jesus was at high tide. Three years of feeding, healing, and teaching had elevated him to rock-star status. The people loved him. He stood up to the authorities. He commanded cadavers and called the shots. He was blue collared, big hearted, and a hometown hero. He was Martin Luther King Jr., Dwight Eisenhower, and Abraham Lincoln in one package.

The crowd was escorting him to Jerusalem to celebrate Passover. They chatted, laughed, and sang happy songs. And then from off to one side, they heard this cry: "Have mercy on us, O Lord, Son of David!" The crowd turned and looked at the two blind men. Eyes vacant, robes tattered, faces leathered by the sun. Pitiful. The people told them to pipe down. This was a victory march, a day of triumph. Jesus was on an important mission. The people would have left the blind men on the side of the road.

Sound familiar? Afflictions can sideline the sufferer. Everyone else has a place in the parade. You would join them if only the tumor would stop growing or the atrophy would stop spreading. Others seem happy. You have mood swings as wide and wild as the African Serengeti. And you've wondered, *What am I to do with this ailment?*

Like Mary, the blind men brought their concern to Jesus: "They cried out all the more, saying, 'Have mercy on us, O Lord, Son of David!'" They didn't ask for Peter or John. They made no request of the disciples or followers. They went straight to the top. They cried out to

Jesus. Persistently, personally, passionately. *I need help. Heal me.*

God's goal for you is wholeness.

Here is why you need to do the same. God's goal for you is wholeness. "Now may God himself, the God of peace, make you pure, belonging only to him. May your whole self—*spirit, soul, and body*—be kept safe and without fault when our Lord Jesus Christ comes" (1 Thess. 5:23 NCV, emphasis mine).

God envisions a complete restoration of the garden of Eden. Everything he saw in his garden was good. This assessment included Adam and Eve. They weren't sick, crippled, depressed, or afflicted. They were spiritually and physically sound. No emphysema, palsy, or paranoia. Yet when they rebelled, everything fell out of harmony. The event is called the Fall for a reason. Adam and Eve had a falling out with God and a falling out with each other. Nature fell out of whack, and the human body fell out of balance. The Fall was exactly that: a fall from wholeness. Sin opened the door, and sickness walked in. "Sin came into the world because of what one man did, and with sin came death. This is why everyone must die—because everyone sinned" (Rom. 5:12 NCV).

Sin and sickness are interlopers, consequences of the same rebellion. But they are cured by the same Redeemer. When Isaiah foretold of Jesus, he described him as the One who would take both our sin and sickness.

He was wounded for our transgressions,
He was bruised for our iniquities. (53:5)

He has borne our infirmities and carried our diseases.
(v. 4 NRSV)

> Sin and sickness are interlopers, consequences of the same rebellion. But they are cured by the same Redeemer.

Jesus treated our sickness in the same way he treated our sin. He took it away. He bore it in himself on the cross. When Matthew saw the large number of healings in Galilee, he remembered the prophecy of Isaiah: "[Jesus] fulfilled Isaiah's well-known sermon: He took our illnesses, He carried our diseases" (Matt. 8:17 MSG).

Did Jesus die for your sins? Yes. Did Jesus die for

your sicknesses? Yes! It is inconsistent to say that Jesus saved your soul but not your body. When Jesus took our sins to the cross, he took our cancers, disfigurements, and depression as well.

Then why do we still get sick? For the same reason we still sin. This is a fallen world, and the kingdom is a coming kingdom. Sickness and sin still stalk our planet. But here is the difference: neither sin nor sickness will have dominion over God's people. Sin cannot condemn us. Disease cannot destroy us. Guilt is defanged, and death has lost its sting. In fact, the very sin and sickness that Satan intends for evil, God redeems for good. Sin becomes a showcase of his grace. Sickness becomes a demonstration of God's ability to heal.

> Sickness and sin still stalk our planet. But here is the difference: neither sin nor sickness will have dominion over God's people.

We aren't victims of rogue molecules or rebellious cells. We do not live beneath the specter of uncontrollable plagues or emotions. Every fiber, molecule, and brain wave answers to his command. He is in charge!

So if you are sick, cry out to Jesus!

Talk to him about your stomach, your skin, your moles. After all, he owns you. Your body was "bought at a price" (1 Cor. 6:20). Do the same with your emotions. Did someone molest you? Did a spouse abuse you? Did you abort a baby or abandon a child? If so, you likely need inner healing.

He will heal you—instantly or gradually or ultimately.

He may heal you *instantly*. One word was enough for him to banish demons, heal epilepsy, and raise the dead. He only had to speak the word, and healing happened. He may do this for you.

Or he may heal you *gradually*. In the case of a blind man from Bethsaida, Jesus healed him in stages. He took him away from the crowd. He rubbed spit on the man's eyes and asked the man what he saw. The man answered. Jesus rubbed them a second time. Jesus healed the man, but he did so gradually (Mark 8:22–26).

And don't forget the story of Lazarus. After Jesus heard of the sickness of his friend, Jesus waited for two days before he went to help. He let Lazarus die. By the time Jesus reached the cemetery, Lazarus had been in the tomb four days. But Jesus called him out. Did Jesus heal Lazarus? Yes, dramatically, but not immediately (John 11:1–44).

Our highest hope, however, is in our *ultimate* healing.

In heaven God will restore our bodies to their intended splendor. "We know that when He is revealed, we shall be like Him" (1 John 3:2). God will turn your tomb into a womb out of which you will be born with a perfect body into a perfect world. In the meantime keep praying. *Father, you are good. I need help. Heal me.*

If Jesus heals you instantly, praise him.

If you are still waiting for healing, trust him. Your suffering is your sermon.

My friend Jim has battled a muscular condition for much of his adult life. The atrophy slurs his speech and impairs his walk. But it does not diminish his faith or erase his smile. On one particular Sunday we had asked members to park in the back of the parking lot and leave the closest spots for guests. As I arrived, I saw Jim. He had parked in the distant corner and was walking toward the sanctuary. *We didn't mean for you to park far away*, I wanted to say.

His life is an example. I pray that God will heal Jim's body. But until he does, God is using Jim to inspire

> If Jesus heals you instantly, praise him. If you are still waiting for healing, trust him. Your suffering is your sermon.

people like me. God will do the same with you. He will use your struggle to change others.

Or he may use your struggle to change you. For two years I have been asking God to remove the pain in my writing hand. Even as I write these words, I feel stiffness in my thumb, fingers, forearm, and shoulder. The doctors chalk it up to thirty-plus books written in longhand. Over the decades the repeated motion has restricted my movement, rendering the simplest of tasks—writing a sentence on a sheet of paper—difficult.

So I do my part. I stretch my fingers. A therapist massages the muscles. I avoid the golf course. I even go to yoga! But most of all I pray.

Better said, I argue. Shouldn't God heal my hand? My pen is my tool. Writing is my assignment. So far he hasn't healed me.

Or has he? These days I pray more as I write. Not eloquent prayers but honest ones. *Lord, I need help . . . Father, my hand is stiff.* The discomfort humbles me. I'm not Max, the author. I am Max, the guy whose hand is wearing out. I want God to heal my hand. Thus far he has used my hand to heal my heart.

Are you waiting for Jesus to heal you? Take hope from Jesus' response to the blind men.

"Have mercy on us, O Lord," they cried.

"Jesus stood still." He stopped dead in his tracks. Everyone else kept going. Jesus froze. Something caught his attention. Something interrupted his journey. We can see him raising his hand to stop the people, lifting a finger to his lips for them to be quiet. "Sh." What was it? What did Jesus hear?

A prayer. An unembellished appeal for help, floating across the path on the winds of faith and landing against his ear. Jesus heard the words and stopped.

He still does. And he still asks, "What do you want me to do for you?"

The duo in Jericho told him. "Lord, that our eyes may be opened," they said.

And you?

Lord, heal this heart condition.

Remove this arthritis.

Restore my hearing.

Jesus' heart went out to the blind men. He "had compassion and touched their eyes." The Greek term means "he felt for them deep down inside his stomach."[2] Jesus moved in where others had stepped away. He healed them.

He will heal you, my friend. I pray he heals you instantly. He may choose to heal you gradually. But this much is sure: Jesus will heal us all ultimately. Wheelchairs, ointments, treatments, and bandages are confiscated at the gateway to heaven. God's children will once again be whole.

six

Forgive Me

Tattoo parlors need a sign over the entrance: "Think before you ink."

Perhaps a recorded voice playing in the background, "Do you really want to carry her name on your knuckles for the rest of your life?"

Or a full-time employee whose singular job is to remind the customer, "The tattoo artist has no delete key."

Professional athletes set the standard for "oops!" tattoos. On the cheek of one NBA star is the letter *P*. He is a Pittsburgh Pirates fan. Only problem—the *P* was stenciled backward. Perhaps he did it himself using a mirror?

Another player tattooed an exact replica of his girlfriend's lips on his neck. Fire-engine red. A perma-kiss. Here's hoping he and his sweetheart stay together. Any other woman is going to think twice about snuggling up to the image of his former girlfriend's lips.

One football player tattooed the word *Gods* on one triceps and *Gift* on the other. Not only was he lacking humility, but he also forgot the apostrophe. He could have used a proofreader.[1]

Parlors can remove the mistakes. For the right price they can get the bad ink out of your skin. Painful and expensive but effective if you want to remove the unwanted marks from your past.

Who doesn't?

You may not have tattoos, but you have regrets. You don't have a souvenir from a Cancun spring-break trip, but you have the memories of one. You didn't embed her name in your shoulder or his name on your thigh. Still, you feel remorse over the words said or deeds done.

Guilt leaves a tattooed heart.

Question: If your unresolved guilt manifested itself in tattoos, how marked up would you be? What images would you see in the mirror? The face of someone you hurt? The amount of money you squandered? All the *could've*s and *should've*s. "I could've been a better mom." "I should've paid better attention."

Dig around in the basement of our souls, and what do we find? Wasted years. Perversions. Destructive diversions. Anger at parents or exes. Selfishness. Arrogance. Racial slurs. We've cheated on exams, cheated on friends.

The consequences can be ugly. Unresolved guilt sires a gaggle of unhealthy emotions. Most of them fit under one of two headings: defensiveness or defeat.

Defensive souls keep the skeleton in the closet. Tell no one. Admit nothing. Seek innocence, not forgiveness. Life is reduced to one aim: suppress the secret. Failures go unaddressed and untreated. Defensive souls build walls around the past.

Defeated souls, on the other hand, are defined by the past. They didn't make mistakes; they *are* the mistakes. They didn't foul up; they *are* foul-ups. They don't hide the past; they wear it on their sleeves. They cudgel themselves with doubt and shame.

Is guilt having its way with you? If so, consider this promise: "No matter how deep the stain of your sins, I can take it out and make you as clean as freshly fallen snow" (Isa. 1:18 TLB). God specializes in guilt removal. He can do what no one else can: extract every last mark from your soul.

When people come to God through faith in Jesus, they receive the greatest of blessings: grace for all their sins. Jesus issues a pardon for every act of rebellion. This grace is a gift. We don't earn it. We can't lose it. But we can forget it. If we're not careful, we can become guilt laden. Even as Christians we need to regulate our guilt dosage.

> Guilt alerts us to the discrepancies between what we are and what God desires. It stirs repentance and renewal.

Understand: guilt is God's idea. He uses it the way highway engineers use rumble strips. When we swerve off track, they call us back. Guilt does the same. It leaves us "more alive, more concerned, more sensitive, more reverent, more human, more passionate, more responsible" (2 Cor. 7:11 MSG). Guilt alerts us to the discrepancies between what we are and what God desires. It stirs repentance and renewal. In appropriate doses guilt is a blessing. In unmonitored dosages, however, guilt is an unbearable burden. We cannot carry it.

But God can. A graphic tradition from the old covenant shows us how he does so.

Three thousand years ago the Hebrew people were

given an annual opportunity to watch their guilt being taken away. Each year as part of the Day of Atonement, thousands of Jews gathered in front of the tabernacle. The priest selected two goats. The first goat was sacrificed. The second goat was presented by the priest. He placed his hands on the head of the goat and confessed the sins of the people. "We are cheaters, Lord. Liars. We envy our friend's success. We covet our neighbor's spouse. We ignore the poor, worship our idols, and engage in evil acts." Down the list he went until all was confessed.

> He shall lay [the sins] on the head of the goat and send it away into the wilderness by the hand of a man who stands in readiness. The goat shall bear on itself all their iniquities to a solitary land; and he shall release the goat in the wilderness. (Lev. 16:21–22 NASB)

The people watched as the guide led the animal away. The pair grew smaller and smaller and eventually disappeared over the horizon. The people waited until the man reappeared, empty-handed. The object lesson was clear: God does not want guilt among his people.

You can bet your Torah that some ten-year-old boy tugged on his mother's robe and said, "Why, Mommy?

Why did they send the goat away? He was innocent. He didn't do anything wrong." The mother, always one to seize the moment, would lower herself until she was eye level with her son and explain, "That is the point, my child. God uses the sinless to carry away the sins of the guilty."

> God uses the sinless to carry away the sins of the guilty.

Or, as Isaiah would write several hundred years later, "The LORD has put on him the punishment for all the evil we have done" (53:6 NCV).

Isaiah did not know the name of God's sin bearer. But we do. Jesus Christ. He came to "put away sin by the sacrifice of Himself" (Heb. 9:26). He "was offered once to bear the sins of many" (v. 28).

If you are in Christ, your sin is gone. It was last seen on the back of your Sin Bearer as he headed out to Death Valley. When Jesus cried on the cross, "My God, my God, why have you forsaken me?" (Matt. 27:46 NIV), he entered the wilderness on your behalf. He carried your sin away. But unlike the sin-bearing goat, Jesus returned sin-free. His resurrection gives us power over sin. Open yourself to the idea of a guilt-free you. This may be difficult. You've dragged around your past for so long that you can't imagine yourself without it. God can. He sees a revision of your script. Just because you were a villain in act 1, you needn't be one in act 2. He makes all things new. "The Son of Man has power on earth to forgive sins" (Mark 2:10). Period. End of discussion. He has the final word on your life. And his word is *grace*.

Jesus did his part. Now do yours.

Give God your guilt. Pray the Pocket Prayer. *Father, you are good. I need help. Forgive me* . . . Tell Jesus what you did. Place your guilt on the back of your Sin Bearer. Give it to Jesus with this request: "Will you take this away?" Do this as often as needed. One time, two times, ten times a day? By all means! Hold nothing back. No sin is too ancient or recent, too evil or insignificant. Be abundant in your confession, and . . .

Be concrete in your confession. Go into as much detail as you can. You're tempted to say, *Lord, forgive me. I am a louse.* But that doesn't work. For one thing you are not a louse; you are God's chosen child, and he loves you. For another, healing happens when the wound is exposed to the atmosphere of grace.

Exactly what is it that you need forgiveness for? For being a bad person? That is too general. For losing your patience in the business meeting and calling your coworker a creep? There, you can confess that.

Confession, you see, is not a punishment for sin; it is an isolation of sin so it can be exposed and extracted.

Be firm in this prayer. Satan traffics in guilt and will not give up an addict without a fight. Exercise your authority as a child of God. Tell guilt where to get off. Speak to it in the name of Jesus. "I left you at the foot of the cross, you evil spirit. Stay there!"

> Confession is not a punishment for sin; it is an isolation of sin so it can be exposed and extracted.

And, for heaven's sake, stop tormenting yourself. Jesus is strong enough to carry your sin. Did he not say he would do so?

> He has removed our sins as far from us
>   as the east is from the west.
> The LORD is like a father to his children,
>   tender and compassionate to those who fear him.
> For he knows how weak we are;
>   he remembers we are only dust. (Ps. 103:12–14 NLT)

We live in a guilt-laden world. But there is a population of people who have discovered the grace of God. They don't drink their guilt away, work it away, or chase it away. They give it away. God wants you to be among them.

The time has come for a clean start, a fresh slate. God does not see the marks of your past. Instead, he sees this: "See, I have inscribed you on the palms of My hands" (Isa. 49:16). God has written your name where he can see it. In the end that is the only tattoo that matters.

seven

They Need Help

You sit in an ER waiting room, surrounded by an anxious family. You rushed here the moment you learned of the accident. The teenage son of your neighbor was injured in a car wreck. He is in surgery. Your friends are in shock. You'd do anything for them. But what can you do?

You try to conceal your shock at the news. Your friend's teenage daughter is pregnant, confused, and considering an abortion. Your friend blames herself. "If only . . . " What can you do?

*You sigh at the images on the TV screen. Yet
another tornado strikes another city. Schools
are demolished, houses destroyed, and lives lost.
Such devastation. But what can you do?*

What can you do? When the challenge is greater than you are. When the hurt is palpable. When you feel helpless and impotent. Where can you turn? I suggest you turn to one of Jesus' most intriguing teachings about prayer.

Suppose you went to a friend's house at midnight, wanting to borrow three loaves of bread. You say to him, "A friend of mine has just arrived for a visit, and I have nothing for him to eat." And suppose he calls out from his bedroom, "Don't bother me. The door is locked for the night, and my family and I are all in bed. I can't help you." But I tell you this—though he won't do it for friendship's sake, if you keep knocking long enough, he will get up and give you whatever you need because of your shameless persistence.

And so I tell you, keep on asking, and you will receive what you ask for. Keep on seeking, and you will find. Keep on knocking, and the door will be opened to you. For everyone who asks, receives. Everyone who seeks, finds. And to everyone who knocks, the door will be opened. (Luke 11:5–10 NLT)

That's you ringing the doorbell at midnight. The neighborhood is quiet. The streets are still. The sky is dark, and so is your friend's two-story house. But still you ring his doorbell, not once or twice but three times. *Ding-dong. Ding-dong. Ding-dong.* It's a big house, so it has a big chime. His Chihuahua wakes up. He has this snappy, who-do-you-think-you-are bark: "Ruff, ruff, ruff."

You envision what is happening upstairs. Your friend's wife is giving him a kick beneath the blankets. "Hank, get up! Someone is at the door." Poor guy. One minute sound asleep. The next, kicked out of bed. Doorbell ringing, dog barking. He's not going to like this.

The porch light comes on. The door opens.

Boy, does he look like a mess. Boxer shorts. T-shirt. Bed hair. Face lined with pillow creases and covered in whiskers.

"What in the world are you doing here?" he asks.

"A friend of mine has just arrived for a visit, and I have nothing for him to eat," you answer.

The home owner grumbles and complains, but you insist. "Come on, Hank, please." Finally Hank acquiesces, invites you in, and takes you to his pantry. You fill a basket with food and take it home. And your surprise guest doesn't have to go to bed hungry. All because you spoke up on behalf of someone else.

This is intercessory prayer at its purest, a confluence of paucity and audacity. *Father, you are good. They need help. I can't, but you can.*

"I can't heal them, but, God, you can."

"I can't forgive them, but, God, you can."

"I can't help them, but, God, you can."

This prayer gets God's attention. After all, if Hank, a cranky, disgruntled friend, will help out, how much more will God do? He never sleeps. He's never irritated. When you knock on his door, he responds quickly and fairly.

> Jesus never refused an intercessory request. Ever!

Jesus never refused an intercessory request. Ever! Peter brought concerns for his sick mother-in-law. The centurion brought a request for his sick servant. Jairus had a sick daughter. A woman from Canaan had a demon-possessed daughter. From sunrise to sunset

Jesus heard one appeal after another: "My uncle cannot walk." "My son cannot see." "My wife is in pain." He heard so many requests that at times the disciples attempted to turn people away (Matt. 15:22–23). Yet Jesus would not let them. "Great crowds came to him, bringing the lame, the blind, the crippled, the mute and many others, and laid them at his feet; and he healed them" (Matt. 15:30 NIV).

He never grew impatient at the requests. But he did grow impatient at the lack of one.

A father once brought his demon-possessed son to the disciples of Jesus. They attempted to help the boy but failed. When Jesus learned of their failure, he erupted in frustration. "O faithless and perverse generation, how long shall I be with you? How long shall I bear with you? Bring him here to Me" (Matt. 17:17).

Such an outburst! Jesus is so überpatient that any sign of impatience is disconcerting. What was the oversight of the disciples? Simple. They never took the boy to Jesus. Not in person and apparently not in prayer. They attempted to heal the boy without calling on Christ. He had to command them: "Bring him here to Me."

Jesus had a strong word for this: *unbelief.* "Then the disciples came to Jesus privately and said, 'Why could we not cast it out?' So Jesus said to them, 'Because of your unbelief'" (vv. 19–20).

Unbelief: attempting to help others without calling on Jesus.

Belief: pounding on God's door at midnight. Doing whatever it takes to present people to Jesus.

À la Moses on Sinai. When God saw the golden calf stunt, he was ready to wipe out the nation of Israel. They were eyewitnesses to ten plagues and one Red Sea opening. Their bellies were full of God-given manna and heaven-sent quail, but did they remember their Deliverer? No, they danced the night away in front of a homemade statue.

God was not happy.

Then the LORD said to Moses, "Go down from this mountain, because your people, the people you brought out of the land of Egypt, have ruined themselves. They have quickly turned away from the things I commanded them to do . . .

"I have seen these people, and I know that they are very stubborn. So now do not stop me. I am so angry with them that I am going to destroy them. Then I will make you and your descendants a great nation." (Ex. 32:7–10 NCV)

Dry grass on Mount Vesuvius stood a better chance of survival. Their only hope was their octogenarian leader, who'd met God, possibly on this same mountain, some years earlier. If Moses had any clout, this was the time to use it. He did.

> [Moses] begged the LORD his God and said, "LORD, don't let your anger destroy your people, whom you brought out of Egypt with your great power and strength. Don't let the people of Egypt say, 'The LORD brought the Israelites out of Egypt for an evil purpose. He planned to kill them in the mountains and destroy them from the earth.' So stop being angry, and don't destroy your people." (vv. 11–12 NCV)

Look at the passion of Moses. On his face one minute, in God's face the next. He's on his knees, pointing his finger, lifting his hands. Shedding tears. Shredding his cloak. Wrestling like Jacob at Jabbok for the lives of his people.

And how did God react? "So the LORD changed his mind and did not destroy the people as he had said he might" (v. 14 NCV).

This is the promise of prayer! We can change God's

mind! His ultimate will is inflexible, but the implementation of his will is not. He does not change in his character and purpose, but he does alter his strategy because of the appeals of his children. We do not change his intention, but we can influence his actions.

> We do not change God's intention, but we can influence his actions.

After all, we are ambassadors for Christ (2 Cor. 5:20). Ambassadors represent the king. They speak with the authority of the throne. They carry with them the imprimatur of the one who sent them. If an ambassador sends a request to the king, will the king listen? If you, God's ambassador in this world, come to your King with a request, will he listen? By all means.

You actually have a "seat with [Christ] in the heavens" (Eph. 2:6 NCV). You don't have a seat at the Supreme Court or in the House of Representatives. You have one far more strategic; you have a seat in the government of God. Like a congressman you represent a district. You speak on behalf of your family, neighborhood, or softball team. Your sphere of influence is your region. As you grow in faith, your district expands. God burdens you with a concern for orphans, distant lands, or needy people. You respond to these promptings by prayer. *Father . . . they need help.*

You are Moses in your cul-de-sac. Moses in your workforce. Moses in your classroom. You plead with God on other people's behalf.

Intercessory prayer isn't rocket science. It acknowledges our inability and God's ability. We come with empty hands but high hopes. Why? God "is able to do exceedingly abundantly above all that we ask or think" (Eph. 3:20). He "will supply all [our] needs according to His riches" (Phil. 4:19 NASB). When God gives, he gives a gift that is "pressed down, shaken together to make room for more, running over, and poured into your lap" (Luke 6:38 NLT).

We have experienced the power of intercessory prayer in our church. In the early nineties, when I was new to the Oak Hills congregation, I had an opportunity to visit Skyline Church in San Diego, California. The minister, John Maxwell, invited me to speak. I agreed in exchange for his best advice for building a healthy church. He was quick to give it: prayer. He specifically suggested that I recruit 120 prayer partners who would commit to pray daily for the church, me, and my family. Upon returning to San Antonio I announced the plan to the congregation. Within a month exactly 120 people had volunteered to form the team. Six months later I was happy to send a report to John.

- We had broken our Sunday attendance record twice.
- We had finished the year with our highest ever average Sunday attendance.
- We had finished the year well over budget.
- We had nearly doubled our staff and elders.
- We had witnessed several significant healings.
- Church antagonism was at an all-time low, and church unity was at an all-time high.

I was stunned! We felt God's wind in our sails, and all we did was increase our resolve to pray for others.

> Nothing pleases Jesus as much as being audaciously trusted.

It's happening again. During the last three months I have led the church through the Pocket Prayer. Our giving is over budget. Every campus is growing. We are enjoying our highest attendance ever. Most important, we are seeing more people come to Christ than in any comparable period in the history of the congregation.

Explanation? Prayer. As we redouble our commitment to pray, God redoubles his promise to bless.

Nothing pleases Jesus as much as being audaciously trusted. When we bring people to Jesus, he opens the pantry. Freddy Vest knows this truth better than most.

On July 28, 2008, this square-jawed cowboy was preparing for his fourth ride at a Graham, Texas, calf roping when he fell off his horse. He was dead before he hit the ground. Cardiac arrest. A friend ran to his side, put his hand under Freddy's head, and began to pray. A veteran firefighter administered CPR and prayed as he pressed Freddy's chest. The friend asked everyone to pray, and the firefighter said he could hear people praying all around him. Soon the arena was a sanctuary of sorts, and Freddy was on the altar. He didn't respond. Forty-five minutes after he collapsed, an ambulance raced him to the nearest hospital. En route his heart began to rally.

Freddy, as it turns out, saw the prayers of the people. "I was with the Lord," he remembers. He describes a feeling of love, more love than anyone could imagine. He remembers a feeling of perfect peace, the kind of peace a child feels being held and rocked by his mother. Freddy remembers seeing the prayers. "God allowed me to see the prayers that came up for me. It started with one bolt of light. And then there were two bolts of light and three. Then there was ten. And then there was like hundreds, and then there were thousands of bolts of light. Each one of those bolts of light was a prayer that someone had sent up for me. And when there got to be so many bolts of light, it exploded into the brightest light . . . That's when God sent me back."[1]

The apostle John remembered something similar. In his vision of heaven John saw the prayers of the saints ascending with incense into the presence of God. Then an angel took the censer, "filled it with fire from the altar, and threw it to the earth. And there were noises, thunderings, lightnings, and an earthquake" (Rev. 8:5).

Behold the power of prayer. You ask God for help, and *bam*! Fire falls to the earth. You lift your concerns to heaven, and turbulence happens! "Noises, thunderings, lightnings, and an earthquake."

Go ahead. Make the midnight knock. Stand up on behalf of those you love. And, yes, stand up on behalf of those you do not. "Pray for those who hurt you" (Matt. 5:44 NCV). The quickest way to douse the fire of anger is with a bucket of prayer. Rather than rant, rave, or seek revenge, pray. Jesus did this. While hanging on the cross, he interceded for his enemies: "Father, forgive them; they don't know what they're doing" (Luke 23:34 MSG). Jesus, even Jesus, left his enemies in God's hands.

Shouldn't we do the same? You are never more like Jesus than when you pray for others. Pray for those you love; pray for those you don't. Pray for this hurting world. Present their case to the Giver of bread.

> You are never more like Jesus than when you pray for others.

And bring a grocery basket. God will give you plenty of blessings to take back to them.

eight

Thank You

I'm thankful for . . .

Andy. He's the dog Denalyn rescued from the shelter. Rangy as a coyote when we got him. He's chubby now. He jumps into bed with us every morning and scampers through the yard like a deer in the pasture when we come home.

Bald spots. I was standing in line at a convenience store when I spotted one on the security screen. *That guy is losing his hair.* Then I realized that guy was me. My bald spot is spreading like a rain puddle. Might as well be grateful. Besides, *bald* starts with a *b*.

Chocolate starts with a *c*. So today I'm thankful for chocolate. Chocolate cookies, candy, cakes, and shakes. Chocolate would've kept Adam and Eve away from the tree and the sailors happy on the *Bounty*.

Dictionaries. Someone has to define words. If d-o-g meant "cat" to you and "rat" to me, we wouldn't know which to catch and which to pet. I'm thankful for dictionaries. And I'm thankful for . . .

Exercises like this one. It was Denalyn's idea. Alphabetize your blessings. Rather than catalog burdens, itemize benefits. The sure cure for the grumpy spirit. A = Andy. B = bald spot. C = chocolate. D = dictionary. It dawns on me that *Denalyn* begins with a *d*.

> Gratitude is a dialysis of sorts. It flushes the self-pity out of our systems.

The next time I make the list, my wife trumps *dictionary*. Which, by the way, is a lesson of the exercise. A person never runs out of reasons to say "thanks."

Thanks. Just the word lifts the spirit. To say thanks is to celebrate a gift. Something. Anything. Animals. Bald spots. Chocolate. Dictionaries and Denalyn. To say thanks is to cross the tracks from have-not to have-much, from the excluded to the recruited. *Thanks* proclaims, "I'm not disadvantaged, disabled, victimized, scandalized, forgotten, or ignored. I am blessed." Gratitude is a dialysis of sorts. It flushes the self-pity out of our systems.

In Scripture the idea of giving thanks is not a suggestion or recommendation; it is a command. It carries the same weight as "love your neighbor" and "give to the poor." More than a hundred times, either by imperative or example, the Bible commands us to be thankful. If quantity implies gravity, God takes thanksgiving seriously.

Here's why. Ingratitude is the original sin. Adam and Eve had a million reasons to give thanks. The waterfalls and fowl, shorelines and sunsets. God found Eden so delightful, he strolled through it in the cool of the day (Gen. 3:8). Adam and Eve found the garden so safe, they wore no clothing (Gen. 2:25). They had nothing to hide and no one to hide from. They indwelt a perfect world. One with creation, one with God, one with each other. Eden was a "one-derful" world. Press your ear against the early pages of Genesis, and you'll hear Eden in concert.

But then came the snake. Satan slithered into the garden. He raised a question about the forbidden tree. Adam and Eve could eat from all the others. But Satan focused on the single fruit they could not touch. "'Eat it,' he hissed, 'and you will be like God'" (Gen. 3:5 NLT).

Just like that, Eden was not enough. It *was* enough, mind you. Ecological harmony. Relational purity. Spiritual peace. Adam and Eve had all they would ever need. God had told them, "I have given you every seed-bearing plant throughout the earth and all the fruit trees for your food" (Gen. 1:29 NLT).

They had their very own produce section. "But there could be more . . . ," suggested the devil, gesturing to the shiny, glimmering delicacy that lay just across the boundary line. And with that thought Eve felt the first flush of discontent. Rather than ponder the garden of fruit she had, she examined the one fruit God forbade. Discontent moved in like a bully on the block.

What if gratitude had won the day? Suppose an unbedazzled Adam and Eve had scoffed at the snake's suggestion. "Are you kidding? Begrudge what we cannot eat? Have you seen this place? Strawberry patches. Melon fields. Orange groves. Blueberry bushes. Let us take you on a tour, snake. We will show you what God has given to us."

Had they chosen gratitude, would the world be different?

If you choose gratitude, will your world be different?

Oh, the hissing we hear. *Don't you want more?* More horsepower. More gigabytes. More legroom. More testosterone.

The white whale of want swims our waters. But God has given Ahab a harpoon: gratitude. So, thank you, Lord, for . . .

F lights, even the full and delayed ones. I don't have to walk.

G olf—that I play it so poorly, others look great.

H eaven. I'll mention heaven this week at the funeral of a baby. The parents will ask me, and I will tell them, "You will see your daughter in heaven." Extract heaven from the human story, and I am mute. I have nothing to offer. Include it, and gratitude appears even in a graveside service.

"Give thanks in everything" (1 Thess. 5:18 HCSB). In everything? *In* trouble, *in* the hospital, *in* a fix, *in* a mess, *in* distress? In . . .

I nterruptions. Jesus did. When five thousand people interrupted his planned retreat, he took them out to lunch. "Then he told the people to sit down on the grass. He took the five loaves and the two fish and, looking to heaven, he *thanked God* for the food" (Matt. 14:19 NCV, emphasis mine).

Jesus was robustly thankful. He was thankful when Mary interrupted the party with perfume. When he hugged children and blessed babies and watched blind people look at their first sunsets, Jesus was thankful. When the disciples returned from their first mission trip, he rejoiced: "I thank You, Father, Lord of heaven and earth" (Luke 10:21).

Thank you, . . .

Jesus, for modeling gratitude. Thank you, . . .

King Jesus, for taking charge, for working all things together for good. Thank you for letting . . .

Love happen. Because I am on the lookout for reasons to be grateful, I spotted love today. The weathered and intertwined hands of an elderly couple in the appliance store. The eager face of a boy catching a ball from his dad in the front yard. Love. Look for love, and you'll find it. Look for . . .

Miracles. You'll find them too.

Rebecca did. She has spent the last three years in pain. "On a scale of one to ten," the doctor explained, "she is a twelve every day." Rebecca's pancreas has shut down. After a dozen operations and changes in medication, no solution is in sight.

Pretty tough challenge. But Rebecca is a tough kid.

She is ten years old. She has fudge-brown hair, eyes that sparkle, a weatherproof smile, and a book of miracles. She showed it to me. I thought she was asleep. Her mom and I conversed in whispered tones in the corner of the hospital room. Homemade sketches hung on the walls. A covey of stuffed animals occupied the couch. Someone had sent a cookie bouquet. I eyed it.

"Mommy." Rebecca's voice was groggy.

"What, honey?"

"Can you show Mr. Max my Miracle Book?"

It's a spiral notebook, edges weathered, adorned with crayoned flowers, stars, and an occasional clown. In the handwriting of a child, miracles:

"I slept all night last night."

"Daddy snuck a puppy into the hospital."

"Mommy is going to place a Christmas tree in the corner."

Her body is in revolt. Her parents are concerned. The doctors are confused. But Rebecca has made a decision. She is going to thank God for miracles. If Rebecca can find reasons to say thanks, can't I?

So the appreciation delineation continues:

Naps. The miracle that happens on a couch on Saturday afternoons.

O h," as in "Oh, it is beautiful." "Oh, it's a girl." "Oh,
that tastes great." I've never said thanks for all the
*oh*s. Which is a shame, for aren't there so many?

P onds: flat circles of moisture.

Q ueens, New York. I ate Korean food there one
July day and met the nicest folks. Never thought
to thank God for them until now.

R unning water. Hot showers. Flowing faucets.
Flushing toilets. I'm never more than a few strides
from good plumbing. How kind of God! Gratitude
turns every shower into a celebration. Nothing silences
grumps like gratitude.

I've read about the grumbling Israelites. "They began
to speak against God and Moses. 'Why have you brought
us out of Egypt to die here in
the wilderness? . . . And we
hate this horrible manna!'"
(Num. 21:5 NLT).

> Nothing silences grumps like gratitude.

Had they forgotten
God's deliverance? The Red
Sea became the red carpet. Manna fell like silver dollars.
They danced the Jubilee jig and carried Moses on their
shoulders. They were grateful at first.

But with the passage of time, ingratitude took over.

So they bellyached. They complained about the room service and pool temperature. It wasn't enough to escape slavery; they wanted manis, pedis, and facials. They turned sour and dour.

God responded with an object lesson for the ages. He unleashed snakes into their camp. Scaled vermin slid through their tents. Toxic fangs everywhere. Shades of Eden. The symbolism is inescapable. Ingratitude is a devil's brew. It will kill you.

> Many were bitten and died. Then the people came to Moses and cried out, "We have sinned by speaking against the Lord and against you. Pray that the Lord will take away the snakes." So Moses prayed for the people.
>
> Then the Lord told him, "Make a replica of a poisonous snake and attach it to a pole. All who are bitten will live if they simply look at it!" So Moses made a snake out of bronze and attached it to a pole. Then anyone who was bitten by a snake could look at the bronze snake and be healed! (vv. 6–9 NLT)

The cure for ingratitude? Look up! Behold the dead snake on the pole. Lift up your eyes! Look what God has done!

The snake is defeated. Look up! The Son of Man has come. Look up. You have a . . .

S avior, forgiving sin. You have . . .

T riumph over death! A . . .

U niverse reclaimed! A . . .

V ictory that no one can take!

God's solution to any challenge is simply this: a grateful spirit. No mist is so thick that the sunlight of appreciation cannot burn it away. Case in point? Jack Ryan.

Pastors aren't supposed to have favorites, I know. But Jack has always been one of mine. You'd more quickly find a moose on the moon than Jack with a complaint. He's a seventy-year-old, silver-haired saint, quick to smile and encourage. Always seated near the front of the sanctuary, lifting his hands to worship from the first song to the final verse.

I went to see him at his home last week. He'd been absent for some time. Heart disease had sucked the strength out of his body. Sleep was scarce. Energy even more so. I sat in the chair next to his, reached across, and took his hands.

"Jack," I asked, "I hear you aren't doing well?"

"Oh, Max," he corrected with a weak smile. "Never better."

"They say you can't sleep."

"No, I can't. But I can pray."

His eyes danced as he tilted his head. "I just talk to Jesus, Max. I tell him I love him. I tell him how good he is. I tell him, 'Thanks.' These are good times for me. I'm just talking to Jesus."

Poor circulation took Jack's color. Disease sapped his vigor. His hands trembled. Skin draped like cloth from his bones. Yet you'd have thought he was a kid on Christmas Eve.

In a sense he was. Early the next morning he went home to Jesus. Who is the real victor in life? Is it not the person who dies with a thankful and hope-filled spirit? How do we die with gratitude? We live with it. We thank God for the . . .

Walks with friends.

X-rays, xylophones, and extra grace God gives when we run out of words that start with *x*.

I read about a lawyer who won a case for his client. The two men celebrated with a nice dinner. At the end of the meal, the client handed the lawyer a fine wallet

> Don't be too quick in your assessment of God's gifts to you. Thank him. Moment by moment. Day by day.

made of Moroccan leather. "Please accept this as my token of appreciation."

The lawyer resisted. "No, I can't settle for a wallet. My fee is $500."

The client looked at the lawyer and shrugged. "Whatever you say." He opened the wallet and extracted two $500 bills. He reinserted one and handed the lawyer the wallet.

Don't be too quick in your assessment of God's gifts to you. Thank him. Moment by moment. Day by day. Thank God for . . .

Yellow-bellied flycatchers and . . .

Zebras.
Thank God for everything.

nine

In Jesus' Name, Amen

IT troubles you, fatigues you, shames you. IT is the disease you can't heal, the job you can't stomach, the marriage you can't fix, the rage you can't tame.

IT hurts.

IT looms over life. Two towering letters, tall and defiant. IT! They march like Frankenstein's monster. Each step a thud. Each thud an earthquake. *Clomp. Clomp. Clomp.* IT! IT! IT!

"Look out! Here IT comes!"

"I can't take IT anymore!"

IT overshadows and intimidates everyone—everyone, that is, except people who take IT to Jesus. People like the Roman soldier.

He was a centurion. He held unquestioned authority over his men. Yet there was something special about this particular officer. He loved his servant. "'Lord, my servant is lying at home paralyzed, dreadfully tormented.' And Jesus said to him, 'I will come and heal him'" (Matt. 8:6–7).

The soldier's prayer was unembroidered. He simply stated a fact: "My servant is lying at home paralyzed, dreadfully tormented."

That was enough to set Jesus in motion. He turned and immediately began to walk in the direction of the centurion's house. But the officer stopped him. "Lord, I am not worthy that You should come under my roof. But only speak a word, and my servant will be healed. For I also am a man under authority, having soldiers under me. And I say to this one, 'Go,' and he goes; and to another, 'Come,' and he comes; and to my servant, 'Do this,' and he does it" (vv. 8–9).

The centurion understood the dynamic of authority. He was a man *under* authority and a man *with* authority. His superiors sent directives to him, and he obeyed. He gave commands, and his soldiers obeyed. They didn't question his decisions. The Roman army respected the chain of command. The centurion knew authority when he saw it. And he saw ultimate authority in Jesus Christ.

> "Only speak a word, and my servant will be healed."
>
> [Jesus] marveled, and said to those who followed, "Assuredly, I say to you, I have not found such great faith, not even in Israel! . . . Go your way; and as you have believed, so let it be done for you." And his servant was healed that same hour. (vv. 8, 10, 13)

The centurion's confidence in Jesus ran deep. Jesus could handle the request long distance. Just a word from Jesus would suffice. Jesus was stunned. *Finally*, his response implies, *someone understands my authority!*

Do we?

Jesus has unimpeachable authority. "He sustains everything by the mighty power of his command" (Heb. 1:3 NLT). "God exalted him to the highest place and gave him the name that is above every name" (Phil. 2:9 NIV).

The Roman government tried to intimidate him. False religion tried to silence him. The devil tried to kill him. All failed. Even "death was no match for him" (Acts 2:24 MSG).

Jesus "disarmed the spiritual rulers and authorities.

He shamed them publicly by his victory over them on the cross" (Col. 2:15 NLT). He was not kidding when he declared, "All authority in heaven and on earth has been given to me" (Matt. 28:18 NIV). Jesus is the command center of the galaxies. "Two sparrows cost only a penny, but not even one of them can die without your Father's knowing it" (Matt. 10:29 NCV). He occupies the Oval Office. He called a coin out of the mouth of a fish. He stopped the waves with a word. He spoke, and a tree withered. He spoke again, and a basket became a banquet. Economy. Meteorology. Botany. Food supply. "All things have been handed over to me by my Father" (Matt. 11:27 NRSV).

That includes Satan. The devil was soundly defeated by Christ on the cross. Jesus outranks him in every situation. He must obey Jesus, and he knows it. Prayers offered in the name of Jesus have "divine power to demolish strongholds" (2 Cor. 10:4 NIV). Demolish! Not damage or hamper but demolish. Prayer falls on strongholds like lit matches on a grass hut.

The devil fears prayer. Imagine this scene. He sat in the back of the room during a strategy session. A dozen demons had gathered to hear a report on the life of a particularly stalwart saint.

"He won't stumble," groused the imp responsible for

his demise. "No matter what I do, he won't turn his back on God."

The council began to offer suggestions.

"Take his purity," one said.

"I tried," replied the fiend, "but he is too moral."

"Take his health," urged another.

"I did, but he refused to grumble or complain."

"Take his belongings."

"Are you kidding? I've stripped the man of every penny and possession. Yet he still rejoices."

For a few moments no one spoke. Finally, from the back of the room, came the low, measured voice of Satan himself. The entire council turned as the fallen angel rose to his feet. His pale face was all but hidden by the hood. A long cape covered his body. He raised his bony hand and made his point. "It's not enough to take his purity. It's not enough to take his health. It's not enough to take his belongings. You must take what matters most."

"What is that?" asked the subordinate.

"You must take his prayer."

Prayer slaps handcuffs on Satan. Prayer takes problems out of the domain of the devil and into the presence of God. Prayer confesses, "God can handle IT. Since he can, I have hope!"

When we pray in the name of Jesus, we come to God

on the basis of Jesus' accomplishment. "Since we have a great high priest [Jesus] over the house of God, let us draw near with a true heart in full assurance of faith" (Heb. 10:21–22 HCSB). As our high priest, Jesus offers our prayers to God. His prayers are always heard. "Truly, truly, I say to you, if you ask the Father for anything in My name, He will give it to you" (John 16:23 NASB).

There are those who say, "Prayer changes things because it changes us." I agree but only in part. Prayer changes things because prayer appeals to the top power in the universe. Prayer is not a magical formula or a mystical chant. It is the yes to God's invitation to invoke his name.

Suppose I say to the manager of a car lot, "I want a brand-new car at no expense." He will likely show me the closest exit.

If, however, I carry a letter signed by the owner of the dealership that states, "Max Lucado is my friend, and I am giving him a new car," guess who drives away in a fancy vehicle? What makes the difference? The authority of the one who signed the letter.

In the same way, when we pray in the name of Jesus Christ, we present a letter signed by our Friend.

Some years ago Denalyn and I happened to be in China on the occasion of our twenty-fifth wedding anniversary. Part of our trip included a visit to the

American embassy and a luncheon with the ambassador. In conversation I mentioned the anniversary to him and asked if he had any restaurant recommendations in Hong Kong. Did he ever! He described an exclusive, members-only club in a downtown high-rise. The words "exclusive, members-only" caused me to ask, "But how? How can we get a table?" He motioned for an aide and whispered instructions in his ear. Momentarily the aide returned with a letter, confirming the reservation, signed by the ambassador.

When I showed the letter to the maître d', he smiled and led us to the table. We dined in the restaurant by virtue of the name of the ambassador.

We access the throne room of God by virtue of the name of Jesus.

Heaven sees his signature and throws open the door of welcome.

Mark it down: IT won't have the last word. Jesus will.

God raised [Christ] from death and set him on a throne in deep heaven, in charge of running the universe, everything from galaxies to governments, no name and no power exempt from his rule. And not just for the time being, but *forever*. He is in charge of it all, has the final word on everything. (Eph. 1:20–22 MSG)

The phrase "In Jesus' name" is not an empty motto or talisman. It is a declaration of truth: My cancer is not in charge; Jesus is. The economy is not in charge; Jesus is. The grumpy neighbor doesn't run the world; Jesus, you do! You, Jesus, are the Head Coach, CEO, President, King, Supreme Ruler, Absolute Monarch, High and Holy Baron, Czar, Overlord, and Rajah of all history.

Just speak the word, Jesus . . .

Pray! Since God works, prayer works. Since God is good, prayer is good. Since you matter to God, your prayers matter in heaven. You're never without hope, because you're never without prayer. And on the occasions you can't find the words to say, pull these out of your pocket:

Father,

> *you are good.*
>> *I need help. Heal me and forgive me.*
>> *They need help.*
>> *Thank you.*
>> *In Jesus' name, amen.*

Study Guide

Prepared by Jenna Lucado Bishop

Prayer in theory.

Prayer in practice.

How do you span the gap between the two—the belief in the power of prayer and the ability to actually put that belief into practice?

After all, the kids need a bath, the boss expects your report tomorrow, and unanswered e-mails are piling up. On top of the busyness, you have questions about prayer and maybe even some doubts. *Why didn't God heal him? Does God really hear me?*

This study guide is designed to help you respond to the teaching in the book so that you will pray "more, better, deeper, stronger." Our prayer for you is that you will increasingly bridge the gap between prayer in theory and prayer in practice.

Every chapter of the guide follows the same easy format, using the acronym PRAY:

Personalize—This is a time to "examine yourself" as Paul suggested in 1 Corinthians 11:28 (NLT). The questions in this section will guide you through a time of personal introspection.

Reflect—In this time you will home in on some of Max's major points from the chapter and will study scriptures that coincide with the teaching. The questions in this section are interactive, designed to embed God's truth deeper in your heart.

Abide—In this section abide in Jesus by doing what this book is all about: praying. Prayer brings us close to God's heart. So take time to draw near to him. You will see suggestions for this prayer time and prayer prompts. If possible, go to a quiet place. Talk to him. Calm your mind, and listen for what he is saying to you. You can write

down your own prayer or use the prayer prompt.
Sit, stand, or kneel—any way you want to pray.
Just be with him.

Yield—This section offers an opportunity to
see how God is nudging you to yield to him.
Yielding to God is the act of surrendering your
heart and complying with what he wants for your
life. Application ideas will be provided, but they
are just suggestions to energize your thinking.

P-R-A-Y. That's it! *Pray.*

Grab a cup of coffee or tea. Write your thoughts in
a journal or on some other piece of paper. Do it solo or
with a group of friends, morning or night, in the kitchen
or on a plane. Personalize your journey through this
Study Guide. As you do it in your unique way, keep in
mind these recommendations:

1. At the beginning of your study, ask God for an
   open heart to learn what he wants to teach you,
   where he wants you to grow, and how he wants you
   to respond.
2. Be honest with your answers. Transparency leads
   to understanding and growth in your prayer life.
3. If you are doing this with a group, answer the

questions beforehand so the discussion is fluid. Pray together as a group. Intercede for one another when you are apart. Consider holding each other accountable to the response ideas that each person identified in the Yield sections.

4. Use a separate prayer journal to write down prayer requests and what you learn about prayer along the way.

May your relationship with Christ reach new heights as you grow stronger and go deeper in prayer.

one

The Pocket Prayer

Personalize

1. Max confesses that he is a "card-carrying member of the PWA: Prayer Wimps Anonymous" while other people belong on the opposite end of the spectrum in the "PGA: Prayer Giants Association." For some people prayer is as natural as breathing. Others of us forget to pray or feel uncomfortable praying.

   How important is prayer to your day? How does it fit in your daily routine? Where do you fall on the following scale? Why did you choose that placement?

Very Little   **Some**   **Often**   **Very Often**

Very Little—I rarely, if ever, talk with God.
Some—I sporadically talk with God.
Often—I talk with God every day.
Very Often—I constantly communicate with God throughout the day.

2. You may relate to this thought: "Prayer is odd, peculiar. Speaking into space." It's often a tug-of-war: part of us is pulled away from prayer because of its peculiarity, while part of us is drawn to it. Based on some examples in the chapter, identify what pulls you toward prayer. Also note what pushes you away from it.

What Pulls Me to Pray:

Difficult seasons of life

Jesus' example of praying

Jesus' promises regarding prayer

A desire to know God as Jesus did

Other

What Pushes Me Away from Prayer:

Busyness

Awkwardness (I feel as if I'm talking into space.)

Doubt in the power of prayer

My checkered history with prayer (My prayers
    sometimes aren't answered.)

Limited understanding of prayer

Other

3. Four brief sentences describe the essence of prayer: "We speak. He listens. He speaks. We listen." Which statement is the hardest for you to believe or do? Why?

Reflect

1. Read Luke 11:1. Max tells us that prayer is the only tutorial the disciples requested. Notice that Jesus set an example of praying before he taught his disciples how to pray. Why do you think he did so?

2. Reread the story about the storm on the Sea of Galilee in Matthew 14:22–33. What did Jesus do in verses 22–23 that equipped him for the impending storm? What does this story teach you about Jesus' prayer life?

3. Philippians 2:5 says, "Let this mind be in you which was also in _____." Even in our prayer lives we can have the same attitude as Christ. To help this sink in, replace Jesus' name in Luke 5:16 with your name: "But Jesus often withdrew to lonely places and prayed" (NIV). God is transforming you to be more like his Son so that you, like Jesus, will often withdraw to spend time with the Father. Practically speaking, how could

you regularly withdraw to spend time with the Father?

4. Max combines the themes of the most familiar prayers in the Bible to make a short, easy-to-remember Pocket Prayer. Look at three of the great prayers in the Bible uttered from different lips and spanning hundreds of years.

Elijah's prayer in 1 Kings 18:36–37
David's prayer in Psalm 13
Jesus' prayer in Luke 11:1–4

Now look at the Pocket Prayer and the scripture associated with each line.

Father—1 Corinthians 8:6
You are good—Psalm 31:19
I need help—Hebrews 13:6
They need help—1 Timothy 2:1
Thank you—Psalm 100:4
In Jesus' name, amen—John 14:13–14

What lines or thoughts within the Pocket Prayer relate to the words prayed by the biblical heroes listed above?

Abide

Use this time to be honest with God about where your prayer life is today and where you want it to be. Here are some thoughts to get you started:

> *Father—You are a Father who wants to talk with your*
> *child.*
> *You are good—Your Son set the perfect example of how*
> *to pray.*
> *I need help—I want to pray the way Jesus prayed. Will*
> *you help me pray more like him? Please remove*
> *anything that pulls me away from prayer. (Tell*
> *God what pulls you away—doubts, distractions,*
> *busyness.)*
> *They need help—Lord, I also lift up loved ones and their*
> *prayer lives. (Offer up specific names to God.)*
> *Thank you—Thank you for teaching us how to pray and*
> *for being a personal God who wants to hear us and*
> *speak to us.*
> *In Jesus' name, amen.*

Yield

- Just as the disciples did, ask Jesus to teach you how to pray deeper, stronger, better, and more.
- Now ask a trusted friend to pray that God will

stretch and grow your prayer life as you go through this book.

- Write down the Pocket Prayer, and put it where you can see it first thing every morning.
- Memorize one scripture from this chapter. It could be Jesus' prayer in Luke 11:2–4, or you might choose John 15:7: "If you remain in me and follow my teachings, you can ask anything you want, and it will be given to you" (NCV).

two

Father . . . Daddy

Personalize

1. Often "prayer begins with an honest, heartfelt 'Oh, Daddy,'" just as Jesus taught. "Our Father in heaven . . . " (Matt. 6:9) uses the casual and warm Aramaic word *Abba* to describe God. But this may not be the kind of father you picture when you think of God.

   What kind of father figure comes to mind when you approach God to talk to him? Point out the lines below that best fit your mental image, or write your own description in a prayer journal.

   A strict father who is disappointed in me and
       points out my flaws
   A dad who acts more like a friend—loving but
       without much wisdom or strength
   A busy and aloof father who has very little time
       for me
   An absent or distant father
   A dad who loves me when I'm good but is
       ashamed of me when I'm bad

A loving daddy who is always willing to listen
and to guide me
Other (explain)

2. Read the following verses. What kind of Father is
God described as being in each?

Psalm 27:10
Isaiah 41:10
James 1:17
1 John 4:10

If you view God as a loving Father, how does
this affect your prayer life? If you don't view
God this way, what makes that concept difficult
for you?

3. The term *daddy* "takes aim at our pride." It puts
us in our place and God in his. You examined how
you view God when you pray. Now take time to
look at yourself. When you pray, is your posture
humble, like a child, letting God be in charge, or
are you more like a parent taking charge? Explain
your answer.

Reflect

1. In the New Testament, religious rulers made a theater out of their prayers, showing off their piety. Matthew 6:5 says, "And when you pray, you must not be like the hypocrites. For they love to stand and pray in the synagogues and at the street corners, that they may be seen by others. Truly, I say to you, they have received their reward" (ESV). What reward do you think Jesus is referring to?

2. Read Matthew 6:7–8. Explain what you think these verses mean.

    Max teaches that these verses point us to the heart behind prayer instead of the eloquence or recitation of the words themselves. What a relief it is to know we can talk to our Abba just as we are, no impressive words needed. How does this knowledge change the way you pray?

3. What do these verses say about Jesus' prayer life? What common theme do you see in them?

    Matthew 14:23
    Mark 1:35
    Luke 22:41

Jesus emphasized getting alone with God, even suggesting you pray in the closet. Does this mean you shouldn't pray in public? Explain your thoughts.

4. The heart behind the prayer matters more than how or where the words are said. Read the following scriptures, and note what kind of attitude each verse points to when talking to God:

1 Timothy 2:8
Hebrews 4:16
2 Chronicles 7:14

Abide

In today's prayer time follow the instructions of Matthew 6:6. Find a room where you can shut the door and be alone. If you are able, take a physical posture of submission before God. This could be kneeling, head down, hands open or some other posture to symbolize your position as a child under the care of your Abba. Below are some thoughts you may want to include in your prayer.

Father—Help me see you as my Daddy who cherishes me and holds me through anything and everything.

*You are good—You are a loving Dad who knows what is
best for me.*

*I need help—Will you help me have the humble and
contrite heart you desire when I talk with you? I
confess that my heart isn't always in the right place.*

*They need help—People all over the world think they
have to be a certain type of person or have to say the
right words in the right place to pray to you. I pray for
protection from the enemy, who wants to rob people of
true, intimate conversation with you.*

*Thank you—Thank you for showing us how to pray and
for being a patient Daddy.*

In Jesus' name, amen.

Yield

- Find a place in your house that can be your
  prayer closet, a place of seclusion.
- Before you start praying, take time to focus
  on God specifically as a loving Father. Maybe
  practice using the word *Daddy* when you pray.
- Memorize a scripture from this chapter such as
  this one: "Your Father can see what is done in
  secret, and he will reward you" (Matt. 6:6 NCV).

three

You Are Good

Personalize

1. "God's goodness is a major headline in the Bible."
   Is his goodness a headline of your heart? Do
   you keep that thought at the forefront of your
   brain, or does it come with stipulations? Evaluate
   your heart, and decide which phrases below best
   describe how you view God's goodness.

   - I always trust that God is good.
   - I believe that God is good when life is good.
   - I have a hard time trusting that God is good.
   - It's easier to believe that God is good to other
     people than to me.
   - I say, "God is good," but my thoughts and
     actions don't always reflect that.
   - Other (explain)

2. Max shares a story about flubbing an oil change
   because of his pride. Many of us make messes in
   life when we try to take control instead of trusting that God is in control. Think of a time when

you took matters into your hands and it resulted in "spilled oil." Why was it hard to trust God in that situation?

3. Psalm 46:10 says, "Be still and know that I am God" (NCV). Take a moment to be still. Meditate on God's goodness and power by reading Psalm 19. Circle or underline any words that stand out. Ask God to let this truth bring peace to your heart.

Reflect

1. "Most people suffer from small thoughts about God." God responds to humanity's small understanding of him in Isaiah 55:8–9. Read the passage. Then rewrite it from your point of view. The first line is provided for you: "The Lord says, *"His* thoughts are not like *my* thoughts . . . "

2. It's easy to forget about or distrust God's goodness. The Israelites were infamous for this. Read Psalm 106. What do verses 7, 13, and 21 have in common? As a result of this , what did the Israelites do, according to verse 19?

What do you turn to for help when you doubt or forget about God's goodness? How does that make it an idol?

3. Stress at work, rocky relationships, disease, natural disasters—at times this world seems more evil than good. What does the Bible say about God's goodness in times of trouble? On a separate sheet of paper, write the promises of the verses below, personalizing them. The first one is given as an example.

John 16:33—Jesus overcame the world, so through him I can have peace and courage in any circumstance.

Psalm 9:9—

Isaiah 46:9–10—

Matthew 10:29–31—

4. "Before you face the world, face your Father." This is the key to resting in God's goodness. The world and the enemy of God are always fighting to be in that "before" position. But let's be like King David, who wrote Psalm 16: "I have set the LORD always before me; because he is at my right hand, I shall not be shaken" (v. 8 ESV). What does putting God "before" you look like in everyday life?

Abide

Spend an extra amount of time elaborating on the "God is good" section today. Tell God which qualities of his character you love, and thank him for the many good things he has done for you.

> *Father—You are a good dad.*
> *You are good—(Tell him how he is good in your life.)*
> *I need help—Help me remember your goodness in dark times and good times.*
> *They need help—(Pray for people you know who do not trust that God is good.)*
> *Thank you—Thank you for always being good regardless of what lies I hear or how much I doubt your goodness. You are the same yesterday, today, and forever!*
> *In Jesus' name, amen.*

Yield

- Max says, "A glimpse of God's goodness changes us." As soon as you wake up each day this week, pause to pray. Then at the end of each day, journal about how praying before you faced your day changed you (your mood, your anxiety, your perspective).

- Set a midday alarm on your phone or computer to remind yourself to take your eyes off the world for a moment and thank God that he is in control. Repeat the Pocket Prayer when you hear the alarm.
- Memorize a verse for this chapter, such as Psalm 34:8—"Taste and see that the LORD is good" (NLT).

four

I Need Help

Personalize

1. "The punch line is clear: *take your problem to Jesus.*"
   When you face a problem, to whom do you tend to
   take it? Which of the options below best describes
   you?

   I immediately take my problem to a family
   member or friend.
   I take it on myself, not wanting to share it with
   anyone.
   I take it to Jesus.
   I go to the Internet and look there for answers.
   I escape to television or social media and try to
   ignore it.
   Other (explain)

2. "Don't worry about anything; instead, pray about
   everything. Tell God what you need, and thank
   him for all he has done. Then you will experience God's peace, which exceeds anything we can
   understand. His peace will guard your hearts and

minds as you live in Christ Jesus" (Phil. 4:6–7 NLT). What part of the passage is the most difficult for you to believe, and why?

3. Read the story about Jesus turning water into wine in John 2:1–12. Paraphrase what Mary did in verses 3–5.

Now think about how you could incorporate Mary's actions into your life. What need or concern is weighing on you? Present this worry to God, and leave it in his hands. Remember, "an unprayed-for problem is an embedded thorn."

Reflect

1. Pastor Dale Galloway says, "Let go and let God." Do you think this means we shouldn't come to God with the same request multiple times? Why or why not?

2. Read Luke 18:1–8. Focus on verse 1. In your own words write down what it says. Whether you present a request once, as Mary did, or multiple times, as the widow did, the deeper purpose of prayer is the relationship it forms between you and your Father.

3. Read 1 Peter 5:7 and finish the sentence: "Cast all your anxiety on him because _____" (NIV).

How does this differ from the following statement: "Cast all your anxiety on him because he will take away all your problems"? Which statement is more comforting to you? Why?

4. Read Matthew 6:25–34. What does each verse below say regarding worry?

v. 30

v. 31

v. 32

v. 33

v. 34

Abide

Spend time with Jesus, laying before him all your burdens. At the end of this session, take time just to be with him and listen for his voice of comfort.

Father—Because you are my Dad, you care about my problems, and you know how to handle them.

You are good—Even in my struggles I trust that you are a good Dad with a purpose for my life. You will use even these struggles for my good.

I need help—(Tell your Father what is burdening you.)

They need help—(Lay the problems of others before him
as well.)
Thank you—Thank you for caring about my problems
and for hearing my prayer.
In Jesus' name, amen.

Yield

- When a problem comes up, practice taking it to
  Jesus immediately, before turning to anyone or
  anything else.
- Continue with your prayer journal. Date and
  note personal prayer requests so you can look
  back and see how God answered them.
- Memorize a scripture from this lesson. First
  Peter 5:7 is a great one: "Cast all your anxiety on
  him because he cares for you" (NIV).

five

Heal Me

Personalize

1. "My God, my God, why have you forsaken me?"
   (Ps. 22:1 NIV)

   "The LORD is my shepherd, I lack nothing."
   (Ps. 23:1 NIV)

   Which of these verses comes closer to describing your feelings during times of suffering? Why? What other verses describe how you feel when you're suffering?

2. Max says, "He will heal you—instantly or gradually or ultimately." Write about a time Jesus healed you gradually. Maybe it's occurring now. What does a gradual healing from a physical, emotional, or spiritual ailment teach you about yourself and about God?

3. Read Revelation 21:1–4. What does this description of heaven do for your heart? How does thinking about heaven affect your everyday life?

Reflect

1. Read the prayer of the blind men outside of Jericho: "Lord, Son of David, have mercy on us!" (Matt. 20:30 NIV). What part of their prayer stands out to you? What is the significance of the titles the blind men gave Jesus?

2. The Bible says that "nothing is impossible with God" (Luke 1:37 NLT). But it also teaches us to be "content in any and every situation" (Phil. 4:12 NIV). Explain how you can have faith that God is able to heal you but you can be content if you are not healed. Or if you disagree with this thought, explain.

3. "Your suffering is your sermon." Max's words align with God's Word. Read the following verses, and then consider what each verse says about possible reasons God would allow illness and suffering.

   Isaiah 48:10
   2 Corinthians 12:9
   James 1:2–4

4. "I gave up all that inferior stuff so I could know Christ personally, experience his resurrection

power, be a partner in his suffering, and go all the way with him to death itself" (Phil. 3:10 MSG). Why did Paul say he wanted to share in Christ's sufferings? What does this tell us about Paul's relationship with Christ?

Abide

During your quiet time with the Lord, talk to him about the pain in your life or in the lives of others. Just as the blind men did, claim him as Lord over the situation, and ask for mercy.

Father—My cry stops you in your tracks just as the blind men stopped Jesus outside of Jericho. Thank you for caring.

You are good—You are good in my healthy seasons and sick seasons. I believe you are the Healer.

I need help—Please heal me from (insert the pain you're struggling with today).

They need help—Please heal (insert the names of ones you know who are sick).

Thank you—Thank you for suffering on this earth as a human so we can know you understand what we feel during seasons of suffering.

In Jesus' name, amen.

Yield

- Write an encouraging card to someone you know who is hurting physically, emotionally, or spiritually.
- In your prayer journal write down a personal example of emotional or physical pain that God healed, and look back on his faithfulness. Then ask God to reveal anything in your heart that you have not handed over to him. If something comes to mind, write it down and begin to pray over those wounds.
- Memorize Isaiah 53:5 (NLT)—"But he was pierced for our rebellion, crushed for our sins. He was beaten so we could be whole. He was whipped so we could be healed."

six

Forgive Me

Personalize

1. What are the two primary unhealthy emotions produced by guilt? Which emotion are you prone to feel? Explain your choice. What other unhealthy products of guilt do you struggle with?

2. Max compares guilt from sin to regrettable tattoos. What guilt tattoo do you need God to remove today? What sin have you held on to for too long?

3. Describe how you would be different if you not only believed you were guilt-free but also lived guilt-free. How would it affect your relationships, your self-esteem, your aspirations?

Reflect

1. Read about the Day of Atonement in Leviticus 16. What verses stand out to you and why? The Bible refers to Jesus as a sacrifice (Hebrews 10:10; Romans 3:25). Does reading about the Day of Atonement impact the way you understand Jesus as your sacrifice? If so, how?

2. Read Hebrews 10:8–10. Now fill in the blank:

"And by that will, we have been made holy through the sacrifice of the body of Jesus Christ _____ for all" (Hebrews 10:10 NIV). Why is the word *once* important to remember when thinking about sins you have committed? How should it alleviate the guilt associated with sin?

3. When people hold on to sin instead of giving it to God, freedom is stripped away, and bondage takes over. Read Psalm 103:12–14 aloud, and personalize it by changing the pronouns to refer to you (for example, "He has removed *my* sins"). Let the truth of these verses speak directly to you.

"He has removed our sins as far from us
    as the east is from the west.
The LORD is like a father to his children,
    tender and compassionate to those who fear him.
For he knows how weak we are;
    he remembers we are only dust." (NLT)

4. Read the following verses, and write on a separate sheet of paper what they say about your identity through Christ Jesus:

2 Corinthians 5:17

Galatians 4:7

Galatians 2:20

Abide

In this time with Jesus "be concrete in your confession" and "firm in this prayer."

> *Father—You know that I am a weak child who is merely dust.*
>
> *You are good—You are always faithful to forgive me, even when I don't forgive myself.*
>
> *I need help—(Confess to God any sin that is on your heart. Be specific.)*
>
> *They need help—(Lift up anyone you know who is burdened with guilt.)*
>
> *Thank you—Thank you for the cross, which took away all the sins of my past, present, and future.*
>
> *In Jesus' name, amen.*

Yield

- If you haven't begun a prayer journal yet, do it this week. When guilt arises from a sin you committed, write the sin in the journal and ask for forgiveness. The act of writing it down may help you expose an internal guilt to God's light and grace.

- If there is someone in your life you need to forgive, start asking God to help you forgive this person just as God always forgives you.
- Memorize 1 John 1:9—"But if we confess our sins to him, he is faithful and just to forgive us our sins and to cleanse us from all wickedness" (NLT).

seven

They Need Help

Personalize

1. Which of these responses describes your typical initial reaction when people approach you with a problem?

   I offer them advice.
   I wallow in the problem with them.
   I pray with them.
   I say I'll pray for them but typically don't.
   I listen but then quickly change the subject.
   Other (explain)

2. If "I pray with them" isn't your typical response, explain what gets in the way of your praying with friends and family (doubting God, frustration with a lack of results, a feeling of inadequacy, discomfort, something else).

3. Max says, "Nothing pleases Jesus as much as being audaciously trusted." Whom do you need to audaciously entrust to Jesus today? Write down a bold prayer for someone whose future seems bleak. Bold prayers honor God.

Reflect

1. Read Romans 8:34 and Hebrews 7:25. What do these verses say Jesus is doing on your behalf?

2. Max says that unbelief is "attempting to help others without calling on Jesus" and that the disciples' unbelief rattled Jesus. It's one of the few times you see him frustrated. Read Hebrews 11:6. According to this verse, how does God's response to your faith differ from Jesus' response to the disciples' unbelief? Read Mark 9:24. What does this verse say you can do if you lack faith?

3. Reread the stories about the persistent neighbor and the persistent widow (Luke 11:5–13; 18:1–8). These stories highlight persistence, diligence, and commitment to prayer. Does this kind of praying fit with the fast-paced society you live in today? Explain.

4. Read the following verses. What do they say about the power of prayer? On a separate sheet of paper, write down the promise of each passage.

James 5:16
Matthew 21:21–22
John 14:13–14

Abide

Spend the majority of this time with Jesus interceding on behalf of others. Before you start, ask God to put on your heart the people he wants you to pray for, and listen for ways he wants you to encourage them.

> *Father—You love these people who are hurting more than I do, so I can trust you.*
> *You are good—You have a plan for those who are on my heart today.*
> *I need help—So much of my world revolves around me. Please help me think of others and pray for them more.*
> *They need help—(Lift up their names and their needs to God.)*
> *Thank you—Thank you for providing this gift of prayer and allowing its power, through your Son, Jesus, to actually change your mind!*
> *In Jesus' name, amen.*

Yield

- This week send someone a text message or note asking how you can specifically pray for him or her.

- If a friend or family member approaches you this week with a struggle, before offering advice, pray with him or her.
- Memorize Luke 11:10—"For everyone who asks, receives. Everyone who seeks, finds. And to everyone who knocks, the door will be opened" (NLT).

eight

Thank You

Personalize

1. "More than a hundred times . . . the Bible commands us to be thankful. If quantity implies gravity, God takes thanksgiving seriously." Do you put gratitude on the same level of importance as other commands from God—commands like loving your neighbor or forgiving your enemies? If so, why? And if not, why not?

2. Satan enticed Eve by pointing to the one thing she could not have. His slithery suggestion that she could have more led to her ingratitude. When do you hear the voice of ingratitude tempting that you could have more (while shopping, watching T.V., comparing yourself to your neighbor)?

3. What gifts—small or big—are you grateful for today? What does your gratitude inspire you to think? How does it affect your prayers? What does it cause you to do?

Reflect

1. The verses below point to some reasons why we lapse into ingratitude. Write in your journal or meditate on some of the hurdles to gratitude mentioned in the verses below:

   Deuteronomy 8:11–14
   Psalm 73:2–4
   Psalm 77:7–9

   Now list ideas that can combat these hurdles to gratitude.

2. Read Luke 17:11–19. Why do you think the other nine lepers did not thank Jesus for their healing?

3. What idea do the verses below have in common?

   Psalm 77:11—"I will remember the deeds of the LORD" (NIV).
   1 Corinthians 11:24—"This is my body, which is for you; do this in remembrance of me" (NIV).
   Jonah 2:7—"When my life was ebbing away, I remembered you, LORD" (NIV).

How could the following words help with ingratitude?

"The cure for ingratitude? Look up! Behold the dead snake on the pole. Lift up your eyes! Look what God has done!"

4. Read 1 Thessalonians 5:16–18. Based on this passage, how important is gratitude to God? How can you pray continually?

Abide

Spend the majority of this time with the Lord telling him those things for which you are grateful.

Father—You are a dad who loves to give gifts to his children.

You are good—Everything good comes from you, and you can use every trial for my good.

I need help—Help me remember to be grateful. It is so easy to complain.

They need help—Help those around me to see their blessings more than their burdens.

Thank you—(Tell him what you are thankful for today.)

In Jesus' name, amen.

Yield

- Write down your own ABCs of gratitude.
- Tell someone why you are specifically thankful for him or her.
- Memorize 1 Thessalonians 5:16–18—"Always be joyful. Never stop praying. Be thankful in all circumstances, for this is God's will for you who belong to Christ Jesus" (NLT).

nine

In Jesus' Name, Amen

Personalize

1. Max, through scriptures and even a fictional
   demonic strategy session, reminds us of the power
   of praying in Jesus' name. It moves God to act. It
   is an impenetrable wall for dark forces. If you were
   honest, how powerful do you believe your prayers
   are? Which option below best describes how you
   see the power of your prayers? Explain.

   My prayers don't seem to have any power. I'm
      not sure they go beyond the ceiling.
   At times I think God responds to my prayers.
   I know that God listens to my prayers and that
      he responds.
   Other (explain)

2. Have you given someone or something too much
   authority over your life? Have you allowed someone or something to rule your attitude, determine
   your decisions, consume your thoughts? If so,
   take this to God in prayer.

3. The gift we have to talk to the supernatural Authority of the universe can easily be forgotten in this natural world. Write down some ways you can remind yourself of this gift so that your prayers are more frequent and more earnest.

Reflect

1. Read the following verses, and identify the name used for Jesus in each:

John 8:12
John 11:25
John 1:29
Matthew 1:23

2. Read Matthew 28:18, Philippians 2:9, and Colossians 1:15–17. What do these verses have in common? What words or phrases within these verses stand out to you by really punctuating Jesus' authority?

3. Look at Matthew 28:19–20 and Romans 8:10–11. What do these verses say about the presence of Jesus in relation to the Christian?

Considering the authority of Christ and that he is with and in the Christian, what can you infer about those who believe (Eph. 1:19–20)?

4. John 16:23 says, "Very truly I tell you, my Father will give you whatever you ask in my name" (NIV). Concentrate on the last three words. What does praying in the name of Jesus really mean? Should it affect the requests that a Christian makes through prayer? If so, how?

Abide

During this time of prayer focus on the authority of Christ. Tell him how glorious and powerful he is, and submit all things to his control.

Father—You are in charge.

You are good—You reign with mercy, goodness, love, and justice. (Spend some time meditating on his power and enumerating ways that he is a good King.)

I need help—Help me submit every detail of my life to you. (Tell him any strongholds in your life that you want him to break through in his powerful name.)

They need help—(Lift up the names of loved ones who have not submitted to the authority of Christ.)

Thank you—Thank you for your lordship and your
kingdom that will never end.
In Jesus' powerful name, amen.

Yield

- Find three names or descriptors that Jesus uses
  for himself in the New Testament, and write
  them down. As you pray, practice using these
  different names as a reminder of all that Jesus is.
- Take time to go through the prayer requests
  you have written down while doing this study.
  Have you seen God answering these requests?
  If so, how?
- Memorize Matthew 1:21: "She will give birth
  to a son, and you are to give him the name
  Jesus, because he will save his people from their
  sins" (NIV).

Before Amen
Prayer Strengths

prepared by David Drury

Dear Readers,

As you've just read in *Before Amen: The Power of a Simple Prayer*, many of the prayers in the Bible can be distilled to a few clear and memorable lines. A powerful, life-changing conversation with God can begin here:

Father,

> *you are good.*

>> *I need help. Heal me and forgive me.*

They need help.

Thank you.

In Jesus' name, amen.

Many of us lack confidence in and are somewhat dissatisfied with our practice of prayer. We wish we prayed more—or more intensely. We feel that other people are prayer veterans while we are prayer rookies. By looking at the pattern of the prayers in *Before Amen*, we can quickly identify four basic prayer strengths.

Prayer strengths are postures—or attitudes—in prayer that we instinctively gravitate toward, postures in which we feel more confident or at least more comfortable. Each of the four strengths corresponds with a core component of the Pocket Prayer.

Worship—You are good.

Trust—I need help.

Compassion—They need help.

Gratitude—Thank you.

After identifying your prayer strength, you may find that your greatest joy comes from growing in the other three areas, which you may have perceived as weaknesses. Using your strengths as a launching pad for more dynamic and rewarding conversations with God will help you become more confident in prayer. You will find that your simple prayers have profound power, not because of how you pray them, but because of the God who hears them.

To identify your prayer strength, use the short assessment tool at **BeforeAmen.com**. Then come back here to read more about each of the prayer strengths and learn how to build on yours.

Worship—You Are Good

Your natural bent is to praise God in every situation. Life has its ups and downs, but if you have the Worship Prayer Strength, you focus on God's goodness. You find it reassuring that, no matter what, God is in control. Where others see clouds, you see silver linings. You don't ignore stark realities; you just don't focus on them. You are always on the lookout for how God is moving in the midst of dark times and bright times.

To worship is to point to God. Just as someone who has performed well or won a ball game points to the sky to honor God, you want your whole life to praise God.

If you have the Worship Prayer Strength, you are sure of the goodness of God, and you share that with people who may be discouraged. In prayer you feel content simply to talk about how good God is. You likely enjoy singing praise songs that describe who God is, and you may have an interest in the names of God or the qualities that describe God.

Bible Prayer Partner

Daniel will make a good Bible prayer partner for you, because he is one of the great prayer heroes in

Scripture. In Daniel 2 we find him disturbed in the night by a vision (v. 19). The text says that "Daniel praised the God of heaven and said: 'Praise be to the name of God for ever and ever; wisdom and power are his'" (vv. 19–20 NIV).

In the verses that follow, Daniel listed what God had done to empower him. Others would be discouraged by being in exile, separated from family and living among foreigners who didn't worship God. But that didn't keep Daniel from praising God for his goodness. Those with the Worship Prayer Strength don't need a crowd to worship. They praise God without an audience and often during persecution.

Building on the Worship Prayer Strength

Worship often aligns with gratitude. When you naturally recognize God's goodness, the next response may be to thank him for what he has done. Increase your Gratitude Strength by thinking about and thanking God for what he has done directly for you. You can also grow in the Trust Strength by asking God to address your ongoing needs, perhaps focusing on healing a specific physical or spiritual issue. Then practice the Compassion Strength by reflecting on the struggles your friends and loved ones are facing. Ask God to care for them and give them the perspective that he is good even in their situations.

Scriptures for Worship in Prayer

Psalms 34:1, 50:23, 95:1–3, 150:6; Isaiah 43:2; 1 Peter 2:9; and John 4:23–24

Trust—I Need Help

Your natural bent is to ask God for help. At first this might seem like a weakness, but if you have the Trust Prayer Strength, you know it's better to lean on the strength of God than to be self-reliant. This is a beautiful place to begin in prayer. If you have the Trust Prayer Strength, you are transparent about your trials, at least with God and perhaps even with others.

To trust is to surrender. We hold things back when we do not trust. But when we pray with the posture of surrender, we pray as children of God, throwing ourselves upon the mercy of the Father. Others might wonder why you let things go that trouble them. The answer is simple: you trust God.

You likely have a unique mix of humility and confidence because of this strength. You can be humble because you know that you don't have to rely on your own strength. But you can approach the throne of God boldly because Scripture says, "This is the confidence we have in approaching God: that if we ask anything according to his will, he hears us" (1 John 5:14 NIV).

Bible Prayer Partner

Nehemiah will make a great Bible prayer partner for you. The book of Nehemiah starts with his prayer journal, and you can build on your strength of trust by following the pattern he set there. He reminded God that he is one "who keeps his covenant" (Nehemiah 1:5 NIV) and that he had made promises to Israel. Nehemiah knew he needed to go before the king and present a huge request, so he prayed, "Give your servant success today by granting him favor in the presence of this man" (v. 11 NIV). Strengthened by his full surrender and requests to God, Nehemiah boldly made his request of the king: "Send me to the city in Judah where my ancestors are buried so that I can rebuild it" (2:5 NIV).

Building on the Trust Prayer Strength

Trusting God aligns well with compassion. When you surrender your needs to God, it becomes second nature to take to him the needs of others as well. Grow in your Compassion Strength by becoming one who speaks up for those in need, even to God. Your instinct to trust God will rub off on those whose needs are deep, so your best act of compassion may be to spend time with them or even to pray with them. Then you can cultivate the Worship Strength by praising God for listening to your requests. Growing in the Gratitude Strength comes by thanking God for answering your prayers. This might include keeping a journal to record the answers to prayers that you've trusted to God.

Scriptures for Trust in Prayer

Matthew 6:7–8, 7:7, 21:22; John 14:3, 15:7; Romans 8:31–34; James 4:7; and 1 John 5:14

Compassion—They Need Help

Your natural bent is to consider others. If you have the Compassion Prayer Strength, you are a natural problem solver, loyal to friends, and sensitive to the needs of those around you, even strangers. You pray for others, but you also match your prayers with action. You think it would be senseless not to help when you can, but you likewise think it would be senseless to act without praying for God to act as well. If you have the Compassion Prayer Strength, your posture is one of looking out for those in need and going to God to present their needs to him.

To have compassion is to intercede and isn't contingent on knowing all the details of a situation. While some hear a request and immediately forget it, you remember it later in prayer. The next time you see that person, you ask how things are going. You sometimes find that you pray for people's concerns longer than they do. You may end up taking care of others more than they take care of themselves.

Your compassion may outrun your time, money, and energy. If you have the Compassion Prayer Strength, you wish you could do much more because you see so much more that could be done. People with this strength commonly rally others to get involved or to pray for those in need. This multiplies the resources.

Bible Prayer Partner

The good Samaritan makes an excellent Bible prayer partner for you. Jesus told the story of the good Samaritan in Luke 10:30–37. When the Samaritan came along and saw the beaten and robbed man, the Samaritan felt "compassion" for him (v. 33). Religious leaders had seen the same man and had ignored him. But the Samaritan soothed and bandaged the man's wounds and then put him on his donkey and took him to an inn. After taking care of him for one night, the Samaritan gave money to the innkeeper and said, "Take care of this man. If his bill runs higher than this, I'll pay you the next time I'm here" (NLT). Today that would be like leaving your credit card to cover any costs. Those with the Compassion Prayer Strength go to great lengths to ensure that people in need are truly helped out of their situation.

Building on the Compassion Prayer Strength

Compassion aligns with trust in several ways. As you discover the needs of those around you, you quickly realize you cannot solve all the problems you encounter.

As you rely on God to meet the needs of others, also turn your own needs over to him, thereby growing in the Trust Strength. In addition, you can increase in the Worship Strength by reflecting on God's compassion. Consider that he knew the cares and concerns of people before you did and is at work as a good God. Then you can build your Gratitude Strength by thanking him for giving you sensitivity to the needs around you and for providing for those needs, even through you.

Scriptures for Compassion in Prayer

Proverbs 19:17; Romans 12:15; 1 Corinthians 12:25–26; 2 Corinthians 1:11; Ephesians 6:18; and 1 Timothy 2:1

Gratitude—Thank You

Your natural bent is to thank God. If you have the Gratitude Prayer Strength, you are content with all that God has provided. Instead of looking for greener grass, you know that God has given you what you need for today. You live in the present, not too much in the past or the future. This makes you a pleasant person to be with, because you are grateful not only to God but also to those around you. While others are blessed and don't know it, you are aware of each blessing that comes your way and have a posture of gratitude.

To have gratitude is to express appreciation. While some think they have earned what they have, you see how everything you have comes from God's provision. This thankfulness shows up when you succeed and someone praises you for it. In these times you are quick to thank God and give him all the glory.

You know that your life is not a mistake. You likely have a deep appreciation for God's attentiveness to the little things. You see him moving in small ways that others miss, and when you do, you know how to give thanks to God.

Bible Prayer Partner

The apostle Paul will make a great Bible prayer partner for you. In his letters to the churches, Paul constantly thanked churches, individuals, and God himself for providing for him along the way. In Colossians he reminded the church that "we always thank God, the Father of our Lord Jesus Christ, when we pray for you, because we have heard of your faith in Christ Jesus and of the love you have for all God's people" (1:3–4 NIV). He recounted why he was grateful for the church in Colosse that was so close to his heart. He shared that since hearing of the church's good deeds, "we have not stopped praying for you. We continually ask God to fill you with the knowledge of his will through all the wisdom and understanding that the Spirit gives" (v. 9 NIV). Paul pointed out what God was doing in and through this church, and his gratitude inspired them in the process.

Building on the Gratitude Prayer Strength

Gratitude often goes hand in hand with worship. Thankfulness leads to a better awareness that God is the giver of all good gifts. Gratitude can be a foundation for the Worship Strength, as worship focuses on the essential goodness of God, who is worthy of thankful praise at all times. You can also surrender more of your needs to God as an act of gratitude and in doing so grow in the Trust Strength. Then increase in the Compassion Strength by thanking God for putting in your path those in need. Ask him to give you his compassionate heart for those he knows should connect with you.

Scriptures for Gratitude in Prayer

2 Samuel 22:49–51; 1 Chronicles 16:34; Psalms 75:1, 118:21, 139:14; Isaiah 12:1, 25:1; Luke 17:11–19; Romans 6:16–18; and Ephesians 5:20

Notes

Chapter 1: The Pocket Prayer

1. For statistics on prayer, see "U. S. News & Beliefnet Prayer Survey Results," Beliefnet, http://www.beliefnet. com/Faiths/Faith-Tools/Meditation/2004/12/U-S- News-Beliefnet-Prayer-Survey-Results.aspx, accessed January 14, 2014. For statistics on exercise, see "New CDC Report Says Many Americans Get No Exercise," Bradley Blackburn, ABC News, February 16, 2011, http:// abcnews.go.com/Health/cdc-report-americans-exercise/ story?id=12932072. For statistics on sexual activity, see "Frequently Asked Sexuality Questions to The Kinsey Institute," Kinsey Institute, http://www.iub.edu/~kinsey/ resources/FAQ.html#frequency, accessed January 14, 2014.

2. "Atheist Prayer: Religious Activity Not Uncommon Among Nonbelievers," Huffington Post, June 26, 2013,

http://www.huffingtonpost.com/2013/06/25/atheist-prayer_n_3498365.html.

Chapter 2: Father . . . Daddy

1. The research of Joachim Jeremias led him to write, "*Abba* was an everyday word, a homely, family word . . . No Jew would have dared to address God in this manner. Jesus did it always, in all His prayers which are handed down to us, with one single exception, the cry from the cross" (Joachim Jeremias, *The Prayers of Jesus* [London: SCM Press, 1967], 57). Some scholars have disagreed with Jeremias. Even so, the invitation to pray "Abba" is reinforced by Jesus' instruction to become like children.
2. Frederick Dale Bruner, *Matthew: A Commentary by Frederick Dale Bruner*, vol. 1, *The Christbook: Matthew 1–12* (Dallas: Word, 1987), 234.

Chapter 3: You Are Good

1. Spiros Zodhiates, ed., *The Hebrew-Greek Key Word Study Bible: Key Insights into God's Word; New American Standard Bible* (Chattanooga, TN: AMG, 2008), Old Testament Dictionary entry #2896.

Chapter 4: I Need Help

1. John Eldredge, *Beautiful Outlaw: Experiencing the Playful, Disruptive, Extravagant Personality of Jesus* (New York: Hachette, 2011), 58.
2. Alan E. Nelson, *Broken in the Right Place* (Nashville: Thomas Nelson, 1994), 89.
3. Helen Roseveare, *Living Faith: Willing to Be Stirred as a*

Pot of Paint (Fearn, UK: Christian Focus Publications, 2007), 56–58.

Chapter 5: Heal Me

1. Philip Yancey, *Prayer: Does It Make Any Difference?* (Grand Rapids, MI: Zondervan, 2006), 266.
2. Frederick Dale Bruner, *Matthew: A Commentary by Frederick Dale Bruner,* vol. 2, *The Churchbook: Matthew 13–28* (Dallas: Word, 1990), 747.

Chapter 6: Forgive Me

1. Rick Reilly, "The Confounding World of Athlete Tattoos," *ESPN The Magazine,* November 14, 2009, http://sports.espn.go.com/espn/columns/story?columnist=reilly_rick&id=4644126&sportCat=nba.

Chapter 7: They Need Help

1. "A Rodeo Cowboy's Fight to Survive," © 2012 The Christian Broadcasting Network Inc. Used with permission. All rights reserved. http://www.cbn.com/tv/1794454498001. The full story is recounted in Freddy Vest, *The Day I Died: My Breathtaking Trip to Heaven and Back,* published by Charisma in 2014.

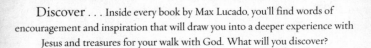

The Lucado Reader's Guide

Discover . . . Inside every book by Max Lucado, you'll find words of encouragement and inspiration that will draw you into a deeper experience with Jesus and treasures for your walk with God. What will you discover?

3:16: The Numbers of Hope
... the 26 words that can change your life.
core scripture: John 3:16

And the Angels Were Silent
... what Jesus Christ's final days can teach you about what matters most.
core scripture: Matthew 20–27

The Applause of Heaven
... the secret to a truly satisfying life.
core scripture: The Beatitudes, Matthew 5:1–10

Before Amen
... the power of a simple prayer.
core scripture: Psalm 145:19

Come Thirsty
... how to rehydrate your heart and sink into the wellspring of God's love.
core scripture: John 7:37–38

Cure for the Common Life
... the unique things God designed you to do with your life.
core scripture: 1 Corinthians 12:7

Facing Your Giants
... when God is for you, no challenge is too great.
core scripture: 1 and 2 Samuel

Fearless
... how faith is the antidote to the fear in your life.
core scripture: John 14:1, 3

A Gentle Thunder
... the God who will do whatever it takes to lead his children back to him.
core scripture: Psalm 81:7

God Came Near
... a love so great that it left heaven to become part of your world.
core scripture: John 1:14

Grace
... the incredible gift that saves and sustains you.
core scripture: Hebrews 12:15

Great Day, Every Day
... how living in a purposeful way will help you trust more, stress less.
core scripture: Psalm 118:24

The Great House of God
... a blueprint for peace, joy, and love found in the Lord's Prayer.
core scripture: The Lord's Prayer, Matthew 6:9–13

He Chose the Nails
... a love so deep that it chose death on a cross—just to win your heart.
core scripture: 1 Peter 1:18–20

He Still Moves Stones
... the God who still does the impossible—in your life.
core scripture: Matthew 12:20

In the Eye of the Storm
... peace in the storms of your life.
core scripture: John 6

In the Grip of Grace
... the greatest gift of all—the grace of God.
core scripture: Romans

It's Not About Me
... why focusing on God will make sense of your life.
core scripture: 2 Corinthians 3:18

Just Like Jesus
... a life free from guilt, fear, and anxiety.
core scripture: Ephesians 4:23–24

A Love Worth Giving
... how living loved frees you to love others.
core scripture: 1 Corinthians 13

Next Door Savior
... a God who walked life's hardest trials—and still walks with you through yours.
core scripture: Matthew 16:13–16

No Wonder They Call Him the Savior
... hope in the unlikeliest place— upon the cross.
core scripture: Romans 5:15

Outlive Your Life
... that a great God created you to do great things.
core scripture: Acts 1

Six Hours One Friday
... forgiveness and healing in the middle of loss and failure.
core scripture: John 19–20

Traveling Light
... the power to release the burdens you were never meant to carry.
core scripture: Psalm 23

When God Whispers Your Name
... the path to hope in knowing that God knows you, never forgets you, and cares about the details of your life.
core scripture: John 10:3

When Christ Comes
... why the best is yet to come.
core scripture: 1 Corinthians 15:23

You'll Get Through This
... hope in the midst of your hard times and a God who uses the mess of life for good.
core scripture: Genesis 50:20

Recommended reading if you're struggling with . . .

FEAR AND WORRY

Before Amen
Come Thirsty
Fearless
For the Tough Times
Next Door Savior
Traveling Light

DISCOURAGEMENT

He Still Moves Stones
Next Door Savior

GRIEF/DEATH OF A LOVED ONE

Next Door Savior
Traveling Light
When Christ Comes
When God Whispers Your Name
You'll Get Through This

GUILT

In the Grip of Grace
Just Like Jesus

LONELINESS

God Came Near

SIN

Before Amen
Facing Your Giants
He Chose the Nails
Six Hours One Friday

WEARINESS

Before Amen
When God Whispers Your Name
You'll Get Through This

Recommended reading if you want to know more about . . .

THE CROSS

And the Angels Were Silent
He Chose the Nails
No Wonder They Call Him the Savior
Six Hours One Friday

GRACE

Before Amen
Grace
He Chose the Nails
In the Grip of Grace

HEAVEN

The Applause of Heaven
When Christ Comes

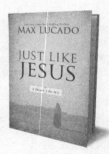

SHARING THE GOSPEL

God Came Near
Grace
No Wonder They Call Him the Savior

Recommended reading if you're looking for more . . .

COMFORT
For the Tough Times
He Chose the Nails
Next Door Savior
Traveling Light
You'll Get Through This

COMPASSION
Outlive Your Life

COURAGE
Facing Your Giants
Fearless

HOPE
3:16: The Numbers of Hope
Before Amen
Facing Your Giants
A Gentle Thunder
God Came Near
Grace

JOY
The Applause of Heaven
Cure for the Common Life
When God Whispers Your Name

LOVE
Come Thirsty
A Love Worth Giving
No Wonder They Call Him the Savior

PEACE
And the Angels Were Silent
Before Amen
The Great House of God
In the Eye of the Storm
Traveling Light
You'll Get Through This

SATISFACTION
And the Angels Were Silent
Come Thirsty
Cure for the Common Life
Great Day Every Day

TRUST
A Gentle Thunder
It's Not About Me
Next Door Savior

Max Lucado books make great gifts!
If you're coming up to a special occasion, consider one of these.

FOR ADULTS:
For the Tough Times
Grace for the Moment
Live Loved
The Lucado Life Lessons Study Bible
Mocha with Max
DaySpring Daybrighteners® and cards

FOR TEENS/GRADUATES:
Let the Journey Begin
You Can Be Everything God Wants You to Be
You Were Made to Make a Difference

FOR KIDS:
Just in Case You Ever Wonder
The Oak Inside the Acorn
You Are Special

FOR PASTORS AND TEACHERS:
God Thinks You're Wonderful
You Changed My Life

AT CHRISTMAS:
The Crippled Lamb
The Christmas Candle
God Came Near

Tools for Your Church and Small Group

Before Amen: A DVD Study

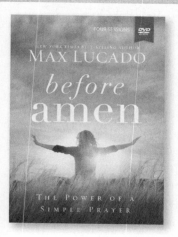

ISBN 978-0-529-12342-8
$21.99

Max Lucado leads this four-session study through his discovery of a simple tool for connecting with God each day. This study will help small group participants build their prayer life, calm the chaos of their world, and grow in Christ.

Before Amen Study Guide

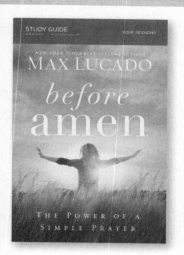

ISBN 978-0-529-12334-3
$9.99

This guide is filled with Scripture study, discussion questions, and practical ideas designed to help small-group members understand Jesus' teaching on prayer and how they can build prayer. An integral part of the *Before Amen* small-group study, it will help group members build prayer into their everyday lives.

More Tools for Your Church and Small Group

Before Amen Church Campaign Kit

ISBN 978-0-529-12369-5
$49.99

The church campaign kit includes a four-session DVD study by Max Lucado; a study guide with discussion questions and video notes; the *Before Amen* trade book; a getting started guide; and access to a website with all the sermon resources churches need to launch and sustain a four-week *Before Amen* campaign.

Pocket Prayers: 40 Simple Prayers that Bring Peace and Rest

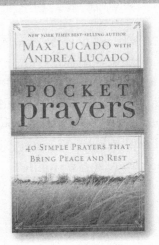

ISBN 978-0-7180-1404-9
$2.99

Includes forty pocket-sized prayers written specifically for times of uncertainty and turmoil. It's ideal for churches and ministries to use as an outreach tool.

Before Amen for Everyone

Before Amen Audiobook

ISBN 978-1-4915-4662-8
$19.99

Enjoy the unabridged audio CD of *Before Amen*.

Before Amen eBook

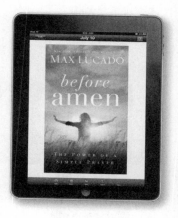

ISBN 978-0-529-12390-9
$19.99

Read *Before Amen* anywhere on your favorite tablet or electronic device.

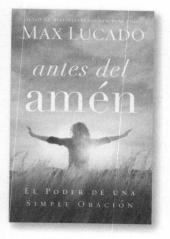

Antes del amén Spanish Edition

ISBN 978-0-7180-0157-5
$13.99

The hope of *Before Amen* is also available for Spanish-language readers.

Make Your Prayers Personal

This beautiful companion journal to *Before Amen* helps readers stoke their prayer life. It features quotes and scriptures to inspire both prayer warriors and those who struggle to pray.

ISBN 978-0-7180-1406-3
$13.99

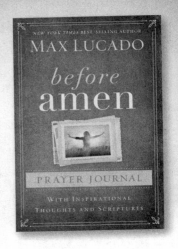

Let your friends and family know that you're praying for them, cheering them on, or praising God with them. Share a DaySpring® greeting card from Max's card line, a Max Lucado Daybrightener®, or other gift item with someone you love today.

www.dayspring.com

before
amen
a worship collection

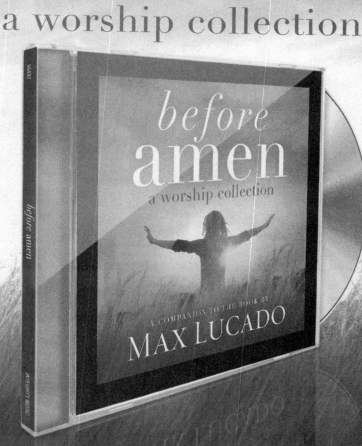

BEFORE AMEN: A WORSHIP COLLECTION is a perfect worship and prayer companion to the book *Before Amen*. Touching on each chapter within the book, these songs further enhance your prayer and devotional times, while helping you memorize and internalize each of the book's themes. The artists featured on this album represent some of the top names in Christian music.

CD: $13.99   UPC: 000768629628
DIGITAL: $9.99   UPC: 000768629659

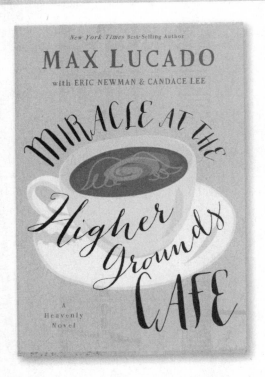

Make Prayer a Daily Part of Your Child's Life

Coming January 2015

ISBN 978-0-7180-1631-9

$19.99

Featuring brand new prayers from Max and Denalyn Lucado alongside classics adapted especially for young readers, the *Lucado Treasury of Bedtime Prayers* will help children begin a lifelong conversation with God.